real PARENTS

real KIDS

real TALK

by

Susan Stone Belton

ACKNOWLEDGMENTS

I want to thank the hundreds and hundreds of parents and children, who over the past 43 years, have allowed me into your homes and your hearts. You have taught me so much and it has been my pleasure to meet every one of you.

I want to thank all the schools and programs who have invited me to bring my parenting message to you. I learn something new every time I speak to a group, and am honored by every invitation.

I want to thank Vandy, one of my first fans and the person without whom I never could have written this book.

I want to thank Hal, the father of my children and a great parenting partner.

And finally, I want to thank Brandon and Casey, my favorite two people. Being a mom is the greatest joy in my life, and I love you both very much.

Table of Contents

Preface

A LIFETIME OF STUDYING FAMILIES

I've been collecting research for this book since I was four years old. That's when, following a two minute phone conversation, I went from being a contented young child living in an intact family to being a neglected child in a chaotic home environment.

When I woke up that morning in April 1962, I was a typical suburban kid, living in a large house north of Chicago with my working father, stay-at-home mother, eight-year-old sister and six-year-old brother. My parents owned a house and two cars, our home was filled with beautiful furniture and numerous toys, and I was a well-cared-for child, secure in her family's love. Right before lunch, I answered our kitchen phone. My grandfather was on the line. "It's an emergency," he said. "Get your mother."

"What's a 'mergency'?" I asked, and he promised to tell me later. Turns out, he didn't have to.

Shortly after my grandfather's call, my sister and brother came home from school expecting lunch. Instead of feeding us, our mother told us to pack a few clothes in a suitcase. My grandfather arrived to pick us up, and we drove away from our home. I went to bed that night in my grandparent's 8th floor apartment on the South Side of Chicago, with my mother on the living room couch, my brother in a small bed next to mine, my sister in an aunt's apartment on the 11th floor, and my father in jail.

My siblings and I never again saw our home or our possessions, and it would be five years before we heard from our father. Overnight, the security and safety we had known vanished, and our status in the world went from being "normal" children with a healthy family life to humiliated children with secrets, shame, a missing father, and a devastated, angry mother. We were never allowed to tell anyone the truth about our father, or forget that we were the disgraced children of a criminal. With our mother working at a full-time job all day, and exhausted when she returned home each night, my siblings and I were forced to raise ourselves, striving every day to prove to the world that we were not criminals like our father.

From the time that I was five years old, I couldn't wait to be a mommy; I wanted to have children so that I could give them everything that had been taken from me.

Fast forward to the fall of 1984. I was a certified special education teacher, living in California, having taught special needs teenagers for several years. And the moment I had been waiting for finally arrived: I gave birth to my first child.

After becoming a mother first to my son, Brandon, and four years later to my daughter, Casey, I continued learning about children and families, both at home and in my career: I taught Gymboree classes—not just a few, but 14 classes a week, for two years; I ran crisis hotlines for troubled parents and teens, and trained other crisis counselors; managed a domestic violence offenders treatment program; provided support for victims in crisis situations; and ran a home-based preschool for several years.

I began to share what I'd learned about children and families with other parents, through one-on-one coaching sessions and group presentations, activities that I still perform today.

Now, I'd like to share what I've learned with you.

Chapter 1

THE TRUE GOAL OF PARENTING

A new baby is like the beginning of all things—
wonder, hope, a dream of possibilities.
~Eda J. Le Shan, family counselor and author

Two things happened in the moment I first held my newborn son, Brandon: I fell fiercely and completely in love with him, and I was humbled by the awesome responsibility of raising him. For the next 21 years, I would be responsible for providing food, shelter, safety, security—pretty much everything—for this new person. Every decision I made as a parent, I realized with pride and excitement, would influence the sort of person my son would become. Of course, I'd known this before Brandon was born, but the enormity of it really didn't hit me until I first gazed down at his tiny, innocent face.

Perhaps you had a similar "Aha!" moment, when your first child arrived. Most new parents do. It's a big adjustment, to go from being responsible only for yourself, to being the 24-hour, always-on-call caregiver for someone who is totally dependent on you. Your baby's care becomes the focus of your life, and you jump in—ready or not—with both feet.

When our children are newborn infants, our job as parents is to teach them that they're safe, they're loved and their needs will be met. But a few months later, when our shock, exhilaration and exhaustion have subsided a bit, and our baby has adjusted to life outside the womb, it's time for us to broaden our focus. As they grow and develop, our children will look to us for much more than just food, love and clean diapers. They'll also need us to show them how to behave. They'll need our guidance and our understanding, and they'll need us to lay down a values road map to follow. And so, while we continue as our child's caregiver, we now add another role, the role of mentor.

As caregivers, we're concerned with our baby's basic needs, but as mentors, we're more focused on our baby's behavior. We begin to wonder, "Should I let my baby cry, or give in to her demands?" "Should I rock him to sleep, or let him cry in his crib as he falls asleep?" "Should I feed her on demand or every three hours?" "Should I hold her so much?" and the big one: "Am I spoiling my child?"

We can't spoil a newborn with our attention, but at some point, usually when our baby is around six months old, it becomes appropriate for us to step back a little. We let her fuss a little bit, so she learns to wait a little bit. We let him cry for a few minutes in his crib, so he learns that he can settle himself. We ask her to wait a little longer between feedings, so she learns that there's a routine. We don't rush to pick her up the instant she cries, so she begins to learn to comfort herself.

As we begin the process of shaping our child's behavior, we each need to consider an important question: *"What kind of adult do I want my child to be?"* We know we don't want a child who is spoiled or rude or mean. We want a child who is kind and polite and friendly, who matures into a hard working, honest, respectful adult. It may seem premature to be thinking about what sort of adult we want our six-month-old baby to become, but after her health and safety are assured, the answers to this crucial question should guide everything we do as parents. After all, this is the true goal of parenting: **helping our beautiful little baby grow into a successful adult.**

Sometimes I wish I had a crystal ball,
so I could see how my kids are going to turn out.
~Vicki, mother of 2 kids

Now that we understand that our job as parents is to raise a successful adult, we can get started.

WHAT IS A SUCCESSFUL ADULT?

Everything I need to be successful,
I have inside of me.
~ Sign at Brooktree Elementary School, San Jose, CA

Success is a complex quality that can be defined as many things and measured in many different ways. As the parent, *you* get to choose the definition of success that you will measure your children against. You get to choose the qualities and values that you want to instill in your children. And you get to guide them toward their success.

To begin the process of raising a successful adult, you must first ask yourself:

"What do I want my child to be like,
when she's 21 years old?"

*I want my daughters to be happy; I want them to be
independent; I want them to love to learn,
to do well in school, to get a good education;
I want them to contribute to society.*
~Daniella, mother of 1 kid and 1 teen

*I want my sons to be happy,
to know what their path is,
to be independent, to be good people.*
~Justine, mother of 2 kids

*I really hope my boys want to spend time with me when
they're grown. I want them to call me up and say,
"Hi Mom. You'll never guess what happened today."
I really hope we have a friendship, then.*
~Ariana, mother of 2 kids

*I hope my children have a sense of happiness
about them; I hope they will make good choices;
I want them to understand
that every decision has consequences;
I want them to be responsible.*
~Paul, father of 2 kids

I want my child to be a well-rounded person,
someone who knows who he is;
a good person, a responsible person.
I hope that my son learns to deal with life's stresses.
I hope he has a lot of friends, a good social network.
~Marla, mother of 1 teen

I hope my children grow up to be satisfied with their
lives, doing what they love and loving what they do.
I hope they feel close to their friends and family.
I hope they realize at least some of their dreams.
~ Adriana, mother of 2 teens

Spend some time thinking about the kind of person you want your child to become. Close your eyes and see her living as a young adult. What is she doing? How is she interacting with her family, her friends, her coworkers, her world? What identifies her as a successful adult?

Now that you've described the kind of person you want your child to become, it's time to get down to the nitty-gritty of defining the *values* that you'll teach your child, to help him become this successful adult.

When Brandon was just a baby, I knew that I wanted him to be a good person, someone who would bring value to the world, someone who was open-minded and kind and honest. This was my vision of a successful adult. The next step was to figure out what I specifically needed to teach Brandon, to help him become this successful adult.

To define the values I wanted to teach Brandon, I considered elements of my own upbringing that helped shape who I am, and I studied the traits of adults whom I thought of as successful. I eventually settled on five values that I wanted to teach Brandon. I would know that I'd succeeded as a parent if, as an adult, Brandon was **honest**, **kind**, **responsible**, **capable** and **close to me.**

Those were some of the values that were important to me then, and that remained the focus of my parenting as I raised Brandon and his sister, Casey, who was born four years later. I knew that if my children had those values at age 21, then they would be good people, and I would have done a good job as a parent.

Let's take a closer look at these qualities of successful adults...

MY TOP 5 TRAITS

Honest

My mother worked very hard to stress the importance of honesty. She taught me to always tell the truth to myself and others, to always be fair, and to never trust people who didn't tell the truth. When I became a mother, I knew that I wanted to raise my children to be honest; I wanted to always be able to trust them. From the time that Brandon and Casey were very young, we read stories about honesty, I answered their questions honestly, and we discussed the differences between the truth and a lie. I was honest with them and demonstrated honesty in my interactions with others. I knew that if I wanted to raise honest children, I needed to be an honest adult.

One day Brandon arrived home from junior high and announced that his coach had withdrawn the school soccer team from an upcoming tournament, because some of the players had been caught taking sodas from a broken soda machine. When I asked Brandon if he had taken one, he replied indignantly, "Mom, of course not. That would be stealing!" After verifying Brandon's story with his coach, I had a proud parenting moment. Brandon had shown me that he was becoming an honest person, and that the lessons I was teaching him were sinking in. Kids who grow up being told the truth and learning the importance of honesty grow into honest adults.

Kind

I feel good whenever I share with those less fortunate, and I wanted to raise children who would feel the same way. From the time they were very young, Brandon and Casey joined me in acts of kindness. We shopped for food and drove it to shelters the week before Thanksgiving. We chose tags from the Giving Tree and bought the requested items for needy kids at Christmas time. Before their birthdays and before Hanukkah, both of my kids donated some of their own toys and clothes to Goodwill. I also taught them smaller, quieter kindnesses: we held the door open for the person coming in behind us, we threw away our own trash when we left a movie or a baseball game, and we each picked up one piece of trash left by someone else every time we visited our local park.

When Casey was 12 years old, we went to the movie, *Space Jam*. In one scene, the cartoon basketball players share a bottle of juice during half-time. When the last player lifts the bottle for his sip, he finds it empty. My daughter looked up at me and whispered, "Oh, that's not fair. I feel bad when that happens." Casey was feeling empathy—for a cartoon character! Another proud parenting moment for me. Kids who grow up experiencing the intrinsic rewards of sharing grow into kind adults.

Responsible

My upbringing forced me to be very independent and very responsible, and I wanted my children to have the same traits. A responsible kid does his homework and his chores without being reminded over and over. A responsible kid calls to check in when you've asked her to. A responsible teen does not do drugs, drink alcohol or skip school. A responsible person is someone you can trust to do what she's supposed to do.

Brandon passed his driving test and received his license on his sixteenth birthday, which was a Friday. That night, when I gave him permission to drive to a friend's house and asked him to be home by 12:30 a.m., he said, "I'm not allowed to drive after midnight with a new license, so I'll be home by 12:00."

When she was 15 years old, Casey worked at a local stable where she was responsible for 45 horses, as well as three staff members, a position that some adults would find intimidating.

I allowed my children to participate in these situations because I trusted them to behave responsibly. I knew they would behave responsibly because I had consistently given them opportunities to do things on their own. Their displays of responsibility earned them additional trust and independence. Kids who grow up with opportunities to be responsible grow into responsible adults.

Capable

I grew up with very little opportunity to try new things. Taking music lessons or playing on a sports team, for instance, were not options for me. As a result, I lacked confidence in myself. When I was invited to go to roller skating, I always said "No," because I had never learned to skate. When I was invited to a swimming pool, I always said "No," because I had never learned to swim. I first learned to drive a car at age 21 and to ride a bike at 24, when I finally had a car and a bike to practice on.

I knew that I wanted to raise my kids to believe they could do or be anything they wanted. I wanted them to know that they could be a musician, an athlete, an artist, a dancer, a baker, a mathematician or whatever else they imagined. My job was to provide the support that would lead to their self-confidence. To do this, I needed to be willing to allow my kids to try—and to fail. I couldn't allow myself to be bothered by messes or mistakes. I needed to encourage the effort and not the result.

Not everyone understood this. My mother-in-law, who was visiting from Florida, joined four-year-old Casey and me in baking a cake one day. She was a little surprised when Casey asked to break an egg, and I handed her a bowl and an egg. "She'll make a mess," Grammy warned.

"Maybe," I replied, "But how will she learn to break an egg if I don't allow her to try?"

I wanted my kids to believe that they could do anything, that failing is simply the first try, and that "It's hard" is not a reason to quit. At the park, when other parents told their kids not to climb too high, I taught Brandon where to put his feet and how to hold on tightly. When Casey wanted to play baseball with boys as opposed to softball with girls, I supported her. Children who are raised to be confident and who are not afraid to try new things grow into capable adults.

Close to Me

When I was five years old, I declared that I wanted to be a mommy. When I was 10 years old, I started babysitting. When I was 26, I finally had a child of my own. I knew that I wanted to have a strong relationship with my children, throughout their lives. I didn't want to be my son's friend (he would have enough of those); I wanted to be his mommy. But I did work to be a friendly mom, so we could enjoy spending time together, talking together, and being close at every age. I didn't want to invest eighteen years raising him, and then have our relationship fade when he went off to college.

So, to ensure a close relationship with my kids, I made them my priority. I listened to their stories and their complaints, and I told them mine. We went places together: to movies, parks, baseball games and back-to-school nights. I volunteered at their schools, always in jobs where I interacted with students and my children would see me. I accompanied their classes on every school field trip, spending time with them and getting to know their classmates and teachers. We watched T.V. together and talked about life lessons. I think

Brandon and Casey grew up knowing that they were my favorite two people (because they were) and that spending time with them was my favorite activity (because it was).

Today, I am very proud to say that I still have a close relationship with both of my adult children. We continue to talk together, laugh together, go to the movies together and discuss everything. Children who grow up close to their parents tend to stay close to their parents. And children who feel close to their parents work even harder at making their parents proud of them, and will strive to do the right thing.

WHY "HAPPY" IS NOT ONE OF MY TOP 5 TRAITS

Happiness is a decision.
~ Michael J. Fox, actor

I think it's interesting that when I talk to parents, so many of them list "happy" as one of their Top 5 Traits. Of course, we all wish that we could raise a happy child. After all, happy children make happy parents. We love our children so much, and we want them to be happy every minute. **But we're not responsible for our child's happiness.** We can teach our children to find things they enjoy, to be resilient and to handle their own disappointments, but we can't teach them to be happy. Being happy is a choice.

The most we can do as parents is to teach our children that they are in control of their own happiness and that happiness comes from within. We also help them find ways of achieving it.

My parents always told me,
"I just want you to be happy."
Sometimes, that's a lot of pressure, to be happy.
~ Debbie, mom of 2 teens

A happy person is not a person
in a certain set of circumstances,
but rather a person with a certain set of attitudes.
~ Hugh Downs, broadcaster and author

If children don't learn how to get things for themselves,
you're kind of abandoning them. We all have
our obligation to make our own way in life.
I think it's important that my daughter knows that it's by
her own efforts that she'll achieve her own happiness.
~ Kelsey Grammer, actor

Our job as parents is to raise successful adults. This goal must motivate everything we do. Once we picture the kind of adults we want our kids to become, and we identify the values we want them to express, we have to focus on instilling those qualities in our children. And we need to maintain that focus all the time, every single day.

In the next chapter, I'll show you how to teach your child to become a successful adult.

Chapter 2

TEACHING YOUR CHILD TO BE SUCCESSFUL

In the final analysis,
it is not what you do for your children,
but what you have taught them to do for themselves,
that will make them successful human beings.
~Ann Landers, advice columnist

BE THE PERSON YOU WANT YOUR CHILD TO BE

Live so that when your children think of
fairness and integrity, they think of you.
~ H. Jackson Brown, author

What's the easiest way to raise a successful adult? Be one yourself! Be a positive role model; show your kids how a successful adult behaves. Demonstrate all those qualities, and live all those values, that you want to instill in your children.

Every time you're around your kids, no matter what you're doing, you're being a role model. You can't escape it.

But you have a choice: you can model behaviors you want your kids to emulate, or those you don't. When you act properly, you teach your child how to do things properly; when you behave improperly, you give your child permission to act improperly. Want to raise a kid who holds the door open for others? Hold the door open for others. Want to raise a kid who writes thank-you notes? Write thank-you notes. Want to raise a child who votes? Take her to the polling place with you when you vote. Make sure your child sees you doing the actions that you want him to imitate.

I try to be a positive role model for my children
by working hard, cleaning up,
being honest, staying fit and being active and happy.
~Claudia, mother of 2 kids

I think I'm a positive role model because I work full time
and yet make time for my daughter every day.
I also show her that even when
times are difficult, you have a choice
to be happy or to not be happy
and the person most impacted
by that choice is you.
~Becky, mother of 1 toddler

I have always told my children
that they should follow their dreams and interests,
and I have modeled that to the best of my ability.
~Mary, mother of 2 teens

I recognize the importance of leading by example.
For example, I value education and the quest to learn.
I love looking through and reading books.
I love going to the library and book stores.
I believe my daughters have picked up
this characteristic of mine.
~Theresa, mother of 2 teens

And as convenient as it would be, you can't just *tell* your children how to act, either—you have to *show* them. How you live your life, how you act, what you do, is more important than what you say. Children watch their parents very closely and learn from everything they see.

Adults teach children in three important ways:
the first is by example,
the second is by example,
and the third is by example.
~Albert Schweitzer, philosopher and physician

Remember the anti-smoking commercial, "Like Father, Like Son"? A little boy and his dad paint the outside of their house together—the dad on a big ladder, with a big brush, the little boy on a step-ladder beside him, with a small brush. They drive together—the little boy pretends to drive with a toy steering wheel, and he imitates his dad's hand signals They walk down the road together—the dad picks up a stone and throws it, the little boy does the same. Finally, father and son are sitting together under a tree. The dad reaches into his jacket, takes out a pack of cigarettes, and lights one up. When he puts the pack of cigarettes on the ground, the little boy picks it up. The narrator says, "Like father, like son. Think about it."

> *Your children will see what you're all about*
> *by what you live rather than what you say.*
> ~ Wayne Dyer, author and speaker

Our kids are always watching us.

Our children are shameless eavesdroppers, accomplished spies. They listen to our phone conversations, they watch us when we think no one is watching, and they hear the things we mutter under our breath when we think they aren't listening. They don't do this to torment us—even though it sometimes has this effect—but because they're programmed to observe adults, to learn the rules of the game of life.

> *Don't worry that children never listen to you;*
> *worry that they are always watching you.*
> ~ Robert Fulghum, author

And so, whenever we're around our kids, they're watching us. They're watching us to learn how to do tasks, how to interact with others in relationships, how to behave in public, how to act when faced with a challenge. They're watching us to learn what to do and how to behave.

> *Children have never been very good at listening to their*
> *elders, but they have never failed to imitate them.*
> ~ James Baldwin, author

> *Kids are like mirrors…*
> *they love to imitate adults, or even other kids.*
> *I've seen my daughter kiss her doll all over her face,*
> *which is what I do to her every morning.*
> *It's very cute.*
> ~Lucy, mother of 1 toddler

I love to entertain and when we have a party and the adults are drinking wine, the girls will open a Martinelli's sparkling apple juice and fill a wine glass and drink from it. I've let this behavior go, but maybe I need to rethink this now.
~Cathy, mother of 2 teens

Because our children depend on us for their safety and stability, they also watch us to gauge our emotional state, to reassure themselves that they're safe, that things are under control, that all is well. If we're upset, they'll be upset, without even knowing why. If we're calm, they'll be calm. And remember, you can't just *say* you're calm, you must *act* calm. You can't fool your kids; they can tell.

Have you ever watched how parents react when their child falls down on the playground? Parents usually react in one of two ways: Either they run over to their child and anxiously call out, "Oh, no, are you okay?" which usually causes the kid to burst into tears. Or the parents remain calm and might even make light of the situation (if it's not serious, of course), which often results in the child picking herself up, brushing herself off, and returning to her play. Our children pick up on our emotions: they become more emotional when we're more emotional; they tend to remain calm if we remain calm.

When I'm with a child who falls, I yell, "Safe!" like a baseball umpire, and usually the kid laughs. Now, if he's truly upset, of course I offer empathy and a reassuring hug. My initial reaction is always, "It's okay," not "Oh, no." It's much easier for kids to cope with a fall, and move on, if we handle it well first. This is true at every age, whenever and wherever our children stumble.

So remember to be the person you want your child to be. Act the way you want them to act. Live the values you want them to learn. It's difficult to always do the right thing, but the rewards are well worth it.

My grandma pretends that she doesn't swear,
even though she does.
~Brianna, 14 years old

Parents should not start a fight with each other.
Because kids will then learn to do that
when they get older.
~Chloe, 5 years old

EVERYTHING MUST BE TAUGHT

I used to own a 170-pound white dog named Polar. Polar knew how to heel on the leash, which was a good thing, since he outweighed me by quite a bit. He would walk by my side, matching my speed and stopping when I stopped. One day my neighbor and I were walking our dogs together. His little dog was running back and forth on a retractable leash, pulling his arm one way and then the other. After awhile, he looked over at Polar, who was walking calmly beside me, then down at his zig-zagging dog. "When are you going to learn how to heel?" he asked his dog.

Since the dog couldn't answer, I figured that I would. "As soon as you teach him," I said.

It's the same with our kids. They're not intuitive. They don't know what we need them to do, unless we teach them. We have to *teach* our kids to be respectful. We have to *teach* our kids to be responsible. We have to *teach* our kids to be polite. We have to *teach* them everything. We can't just expect them to know how to behave. We wouldn't hand a violin to a four-year-old who'd never had music lessons, and expect him to play a sonata. So why would we expect our kids to be good people if we don't teach them how to be good people?

It's never too early to start teaching our kids how to behave. Remember when our little babies would hold up those gummy graham crackers that they were chewing on, to give us a bite? When we smiled at them and said, "Thank you for sharing. That's so nice!", we were teaching them that sharing is good.

> ***It doesn't matter how old you are,***
> ***you should always share.***
> ~Rebecca, 5 years old

From the back seat of my car, seven-year-old Anna piped up, "Carl won't share." Anna's five-year-old brother had taken the bag of pretzels and apparently would not loosen his grip on them. I could have ordered Carl to share or I could have raised my voice to a threatening tone. Instead, I simply said, "Oh, of course he will share. Nice people share, and Carl is a nice boy." A quick peek in my rear view mirror a moment later revealed two children happily eating pretzels. Carl heard my high expectations and he chose to live up to my expectation of doing the right thing.

Teach your child before he needs to do it alone.

Give a man a fish and you feed him for a day.
Teach a man to fish and you feed him for a lifetime.
~Chinese Proverb

Not only do we need to teach our children everything, but we also need to begin teaching them how to use these life skills *before* they need to do them on their own. If you want your kids to be confident in their own values—honest and kind and responsible and capable—you need to start teaching them how to be that way when they're little, even as young as two years old. Not only will they have many years to practice their skills, but since we never know when each skill will be needed, it gives our children—and ourselves—confidence that they'll be ready when situations arise.

Teaching our children to look
both ways before crossing the street,
when they were young,
has come in very handy,
now that they're older.
~Samantha, mom of 3 kids

LAY DOWN A
VALUES ROAD MAP

*It's not hard to make decisions
when you know what your values are.*
~Roy Disney, Walt Disney Executive

When we teach our kids our values, we are laying down a Values Road Map to help guide them through life. This road map gives them direction so that when they face dilemmas and challenges, they can ask, "What did my parents teach me?" They might step off that Values Road Map now and then, or they might not follow the exact path we lay down for them, but at least they have a path to follow, which is the foundation of a successful life.

*Children are not casual guests in our home.
They have been loaned to us temporarily
for the purpose of loving them
and instilling a foundation of values
on which their future lives will be built.*
~ Dr. James C. Dobson, founder of "Focus on the Family"

What values should I teach my children?

The short answer is: you should teach your children the values that you believe will help them to become the type of person you want them to be.

Ideally, parenting partners will discuss which values they want to instill in their children, and then institute these as their "family values." These family values will be the foundation of their children's Values Road Map, guiding them toward their successful future.

What are some of your family's values?

The values I teach my children are:
honesty, hard work,
responsibility,
politeness and teamwork.
~ Margaret, mother of 1 toddler and 2 kids

Some of the values I teach my daughters are:
respect, integrity,
trust, discipline,
loyalty and family.
~Anita, mother of 1 kid and 1 teen

It is still early, but we are trying to teach our daughter to have good manners, to respect her elders, to behave in church, and to share and play with people of all ages and backgrounds.
~ Stephanie, mother of 1 toddler

Our family values include honesty, compassion toward all life, kindness, trust, and a willingness to pitch in.
- Bob, father of 2 teens

ALLOW YOUR KIDS TO BE DISAPPOINTED SOMETIMES

Another valuable lesson to teach our kids is how to deal with disappointment. Sometimes things won't go our kids' way, and they'll be disappointed. They'll need to know how to deal with that disappointment, and it's our job to teach them. As adults, we have to deal with our own disappointment. No one helps us with that. We might talk with a friend, but we need to handle our disappointment ourselves.

Successful adults know how to handle disappointment: they don't stomp around, or punch holes in the wall, or throw themselves down and have a tantrum, or shout obscenity-laden diatribes, or throw things, or hurt people they're mad at (even if they want to). So when your two-year-old says, "Can I have a cookie?" and you say, "No," and he falls on the ground and cries and has a full-on tantrum, you can think, "Yes! I'm teaching him to be a successful adult. I'm letting him experience some disappointment and learn how to deal with it."

Children of all ages need to learn to handle their disappointment. Soccer moms and dads will especially appreciate this story...

One Saturday morning, I was in the grocery store's checkout line behind a woman who was buying a case of juice boxes and a box of granola bars. I said, "Oh, you must be going to a soccer game."

Well, the woman was not in a good mood. She turned around and snapped, "Yes, the snack mom forgot to bring snacks, and I had to leave the game to drive over here to get snacks for the team."

I leaned back a little and said, "Whoa, sorry I asked." An angry soccer mom needs to be left alone.

What would have happened if that team of young soccer players had come off the field and the parents had said, "Sorry, no snack today"? Would they have been disappointed? Sure. For how long? Maybe for a few minutes. Then, they would have gotten over it and carried on with their day.

What a great lesson it would have been, if the parents had then said, "We're sorry you're disappointed, but it's important to remember that if you promise to do something, you've really got to do it because other people might be disappointed if you don't follow through with your promises."

Wouldn't that have been an amazing learning moment for those kids? Instead, they got one more juice box and a granola bar, same as always.

We have to let our kids be disappointed sometimes. They have to fail at something or feel sad in order to learn how to be resilient. Resiliency is a very good quality, but it's not easy for us to let our kids experience disappointment. We love our children so much, we have such intense feelings for them, that we never want them to experience even a moment of pain.

One of the things I like least about parenting,
is when I feel helpless to fix my kids
when they're broken.
~Rachel, mother of 2 teens

We want to fix everything for our kids, but we can't. Even if we could, we shouldn't, because they need to learn to deal with disappointment, in order to become successful adults.

When your child comes home and says, "I wasn't invited to Billy's birthday party," you could get on the phone and call Billy's mom, but you shouldn't, no matter how much you may want to. A better lesson for your child would be for you to say, "I'm so sorry you weren't invited. That must be disappointing."

When our kids become teenagers, they're disappointed a lot. They don't make the team; they don't make first chair in the orchestra; the girl they invite to the prom turns them down. We're not usually there to help them when it happens. They've got to be able to handle that disappointment on their own. If they learn to deal with disappointment when they're younger, they'll have a head start.

A great question you can ask your kids when they're feeling sad or feeling bad is, "What can you do to make yourself feel better?" Not, "What can Mommy and Daddy do?" but "What can *you* do to make yourself feel better?" Kids need to learn to do this for themselves, because successful adults figure out how to make themselves feel better. Of course we offer our kids a hug, reassurance, empathy and a listening ear, but we cannot—and should not—always offer a solution.

ASSIGN CHORES TO KIDS OF EVERY AGE

My mother never allowed me to make my bed—
she said I wouldn't do it right.
So when I became an adult, it was very hard for me
to do things like make beds and do the dishes.
~Bella, 84-year-old great-grandmother

Chores are a great tool for teaching our children to be successful adults. I felt that my children needed, as adults, to be able to mow the lawn, do laundry, cook a real meal and change a light bulb. As their parent, it was up to me to teach them how to do these tasks, and more. To accomplish this, I began giving my kids chores when they were very young, so they would get used to the idea of helping out around the house and they would learn how to perform useful tasks. I wanted them to grow up with chores as a normal and expected part of life

We have started assigning tasks, to see
which ones are best suited for our child.
If he doesn't do his chores,
his videos will be taken away.
~Irina, mother of 1 kid

Children who have been raised doing chores usually do them with less complaining and resistance than children who haven't. NOT teaching your children how to do household chores is a disservice to your children—and to their future spouses.

Our kids are expected to help out around the house.
They do their own laundry, set and clear the table,
take out the garbage and recycling, take care of the
family cat and pick up after themselves
(with a little prodding).
~Paul, father of 2 teens

I have a posted list of chores that I have to do every day.
If I do all my chores for the day, I can watch TV;
if I don't, I can't.
~Rebecca, 13 years old

Completing chores makes children feel proud, confident, independent and capable—all traits of a successful adult. Being assigned chores shows kids that they're a necessary and important part of a team and that we trust them. Doing chores also helps children understand how much work it takes to maintain the home. Simply start by giving your kids easy chores when they're little—have them throw their laundry in the hamper, help set the table and hang up their wet towels—and give them more complex jobs as they get older.

We don't have assigned chores,
but my parents ask me to help out sometimes.
~Carla, 14 years old

I think it's better to have no chores,
and have your parents ask you to do things,
because if you have chores, you're going to be reluctant
and not want to do them.
~Angela, 13 years old

I used to have chores, but now I tell my parents
I have too much homework,
so I don't have to do them anymore.
That's my excuse.
~Barry, 14 years old

My little sister doesn't have to do chores, but I do.
I think that's unfair!
~Steven, 14 years old

My oldest son absolutely hates putting away his laundry.
I hate unloading the dishwasher.
So, I fold and put away his laundry;
he unloads the dishwasher.
We are both happier that way.
It's a compromise that really works for me.
~Melanie, mother of 2 toddlers and 2 kids

I find it hard to give the kids
too many chores during the school week,
since they're so busy
with school work and other activities.
~Wendy, mother of 1 kid and 1 teen

I tend to just give them random chores
depending on my mood.
My daughter now has to do her own laundry,
which is wonderful!
~Kelly, mother of 2 teens

Sometimes my son whines and tells us how we are
terrible, mean parents for making him do chores
he does not want to do.
This makes me, personally, hit the roof.
~Ariana, mother of 1 toddler and 1 kid

I have to say that I am sometimes
lax about their chores,
because I feel they are so busy
with school, sports and activities,
that there isn't enough time
in the day.
~Lucy, mother of 2 teens

We don't have chores!
I believe this is a battle not worth having!
~Andrea, mother of 2 kids and 1 teen

FOLLOWING YOUR OWN LEAD: IGNORING THE PEANUT GALLERY

To think is easy. To act is difficult.
To act as one thinks is the most difficult.
~Johann Wolfgang von Goethe, author

Now you're all set to be a terrific parent, right? You know that your child is always watching you, learning how to behave, so you make sure that you're a fabulous role model; you know that everything must be taught, so you make sure that you teach your child every chance you get; you know that in order to give your child a guide to successful living, you've got to set him up with a values road map; and you know that in order to help prepare your child to be a self-sufficient adult, you've got to teach her how to do things on her own . Great!

But then your mother says, "You really shouldn't let Sammy stay up so late," or your next door neighbor scowls at you when you allow your toddler to have a tantrum right there in the front yard, or all the other parents (it seems) allow their preteen kids to watch R-rated movies (you don't), or your coworkers can't believe you make your twelve-year-old daughter *do her own laundry,* and suddenly, your fledgling confidence in your new-found parenting skills is shaken. You begin to doubt that you actually *do* know what you're doing.

We've all experienced this deluge of advice and opinions (disguised as superior knowledge) from other people. For different reasons, these people—sometimes well-meaning, sometimes not—feel compelled to offer their solutions to your parenting issues, or tout their own parenting methods as being "The Right Way," or who say nothing but shoot looks your way that say volumes. I like to refer to these people as The Peanut Gallery.

Don't let other people tell you what you want.
~Pat Riley, professional basketball coach

Every once in awhile, I have insecure moments when I doubt myself. It's just so good to know that we all go through that.
~Emily, mother of 2 teens

I'm so thankful when another mom empathizes with me: "I know how you feel."
~Tania, mother of 2 kids

I've had my fair share of parenting issues over the years,
and I've learned to just find peace in the situations.
Many times, I've wanted a big hole to open up and
swallow me, so I could disappear.
~Cathy, mother of 3 kids

It's not helpful, when you're having parenting troubles,
to have someone tell you their little darling is perfect.
I want someone to tell me it's going to be all right,
that this is just a phase.
~Becky, mother of 2 kids

Everyone, it seems, has an opinion about how others should parent. In-laws, grandparents, aunts and uncles, neighbors, other parents, the media, the church or synagogue, the neighborhood and community we live in...all want to have a say in how we raise our children. But remember this: only Mom and Dad can decide what values and lessons they want to teach their own children, and how they want to teach them.

You can't judge another parent's parenting,
because you can't know their kids and their situation.
It's all different.
~Judy, mother of 2 teens

Many families live in a multi-generational home. It can be particularly hard to stick to your parenting style when others in the same house are critiquing you and your children. It can also be difficult when we're in a public place with our children and they do something that others find annoying. We know, or at least feel, that we are being watched to see how we will respond, and we'll then be judged by our response.

I think we are all guilty of worrying
about being judged by others.
To be truthful, I think we are our own worst enemy.
~Maggie, mother of 2 kids

I think a lot of us have this expectation of ourselves,
wanting to be like everybody else.
~Laura, mother 1 kid

Often we might be tempted to do something, or say something, to our children because we feel that someone else expects us to. We should resist these temptations at all costs! Parenting according to other people's expectations is an especially arbitrary way to raise our children. Our kids don't need parenting from The Peanut Gallery, they need parenting from *us*, and that means they need us to be consistent, to be honest, to be ourselves. We need to rely on our *own* values, stick to our *own* opinions, and make our *own* judgments in order to be fair to our children. Parenting to make others happy might work in the short-term, by allowing us to dodge some criticism, but it sure doesn't work in the long-run for us or for our kids.

My son loves to play violent video games,
which concerned me. So I told him,
"This is how we're going to do it...
You rent the game,
we'll look at it together,
and I'll decide whether it's suitable."
I know other moms might look at me and disagree,
but in our situation, it works.
~Tara, mother of 1 kid

We're all real people.
I just hate how we moms judge each other,
instead of supporting each other.
~Anne, mother of 3 kids

As parents, it's our responsibility to teach our children how to be successful. To accomplish this, we need to be positive role models, demonstrating how successful adults behave; we have to instill in our children the values that will guide them on the path toward their goals; we need to allow them to experience disappointment sometimes, so they can learn resilience; and we should assign them chores, so they can gain some responsibility and practice the skills they'll need to know, as successful adults. And after all this, we need to hold firm when the Peanut Gallery tries to impose their will on us, and sway us from our course.

In the next chapter, you'll learn why your kids behave the way they do, and how working with your children's innate behaviors can make you a better parent.

Chapter 3

UNDERSTANDING YOUR CHILD

To be a conscious parent, and really look to that
little being's mental and physical health,
is a responsibility which most of us, including me,
avoid most of the time because it's too hard.
~John Lennon, musician

During the 40-plus years that I've been working with families, I've learned quite a lot about parents, kids, and the interactions between them. What became clear is that as parents, we need to understand our children before we can truly know how to get along with them. Once we understand our kids, then knowing how and when to talk with them, what to say to them, and how to best interact with them, become more intuitive.

In this chapter, I'll share some concepts that will help you better understand your child, and should make your job as a parent easier and more fun.

LOVE YOUR KIDS
FOR WHO THEY ARE

Children aren't coloring books.
You don't get to fill them with your favorite colors.
~ Khaled Hosseini, in *The Kite Runner*

Have you ever looked at your child and thought, "Who are you? Where did you come from?" Maybe you've wondered, "Where did you get that trait?" If you have, then you're in good company. Many parents are baffled from time to time by their kids' personality or behavior.

Before I had my first child,
my friends threw me a shower.
There were lots of baby pictures
and all the babies were cute and happy.
Then, when my daughter was born,
she cried all the time, and I thought,
"What is this? This can't be good."
My daughter is sixteen now, and I'm still recovering.
~Beth, mother of 2 teens

When our children are babies, we tend to create little mental pictures of how we expect they'll be. Not just whether they'll grow up to be a doctor or a lawyer or a stock broker, but also how their personalities might be. Then, when our children begin to grow up, and they begin to express their personalities, sometimes they differ from those pretty little pictures we've carried around in our head: They're louder than we thought they'd be; they're quieter than we thought they'd be. They're into sports instead of music; they're into music instead of sports. They're more shy or more outgoing than we thought they'd be. Maybe our kid is a painter when we hoped for a scientist, or a techie when we hoped for a writer.

We inevitably doom our children to failure and frustration when we try to set their goals for them.
Dr. Jess Lair, professor and philosopher

If our kids are different from what we expected, there's not much we can do about it. We can modify our children's behavior, but we can't change their personalities. And we shouldn't try. Our kids are who they are; they need us to love them unconditionally, and to accept their personality, quirks and all.

You can choose your friends,
but you can't choose your family.
~Anonymous

Let's admit it: we may not like everything about our children. Our kids may have traits we dislike in our partners. Or, our kids may have traits that we dislike in ourselves. Or, our kids may have traits that we dislike in other people. That's just how it goes. And as their parents, we'll love them anyway. (By the way, you'll be a lot happier if you focus more on the traits that you *like* in your kids, than on the ones you don't.)

Remember, we're raising individuals, not clones. Are you exactly like your parents? Probably not. Do you want to raise kids who are exactly like you? Hopefully not. You want to raise kids who are exactly how *they* want to be, exactly who they are *meant* to be.

Some parents view their child as a piece of stone that they can carve into exactly the person they want them to be. They try to chisel and chip away all the parts of their child's personality that they don't like, until their child matches the parents' mental picture. This seldom, if ever, turns out well.

I don't think kids are pieces of stone that can be carved. I think they're clumps of clay that can be molded and shaped. By providing constant support and encouragement, parents can help shape their children, so they always fit comfortably into their own unique design.

Children are like wet cement.
Whatever falls on them makes an impression.
~Dr. Haim Ginott, child psychologist

We have to let our kids be themselves. Part of growing up is figuring out how to be an individual, how to find our own place in the family, and in the world. It's vital for their well-being that our kids know we will love them every step of the way, no matter what.

I get bogged down in the negative, sometimes,
and it's really hard to see the positive.
Sometimes, it's hard for us; as parents, we tend to focus
in on that one negative thing,
and forget about all their really nice qualities.
~Theresa, mother of 2 teens

I feel very much a lack of control over my children.
It's not that I want to control them, but I feel like
there is so much uncertainty in the world
and their own personalities. With my kids,
they're so unpredictable, that it makes me want to
disavow any responsibility for how they turn out.
~Monica, mother of 3 kids

My child is just starting to exert her own personality
and opinions about things. It comes as a shock
because she was such an easy baby...
but it's also neat to see her
grow up and become her own person.
~Laura, mother of 1 toddler

❖

It's hard when you have a disagreeable child.
I have had to learn to separate myself from it, and try to
find the best way to help him overcome his bad attitude.
I have to remind myself that I, too, have bad days
and can't be expected to always "put on a happy face".
~Michelle, mother of 1 baby and 3 kids

Why is it, that when you have two or more children, their personalities are often totally different from each other? Just when you think you have the whole parenting thing figured out, you have a second child and have to start the learning process all over again.

It's hard if the child is different from what we expected,
but we've gotten better at understanding
each of our children's different personalities
and both accepting them and working with them.
~Barbara, mother of 1 toddler and 2 kids

I got my easy child first. From the day he was born, Brandon was an easy-going baby. As a toddler, when he would attempt to touch something that was off limits, I would say, "Please don't touch that," and he wouldn't touch it again. I never needed to use safety latches, baby gates, or doorknob covers. That was the personality he was born with, and as a young adult, he is still one of the most laid-back, easygoing people I've ever known.

My second child was born independent and defiant, and tested every limit I gave her. After Casey was born, our home became Fort Knox, defended with gates, latches, and empty lower shelves. As a toddler, Casey took it as a challenge to see how many times she could touch something that she'd been told not to touch.

In addition to having a completely different personality from Brandon, Casey needed to be different from her brother, to mark her place in our family and in her world. In order to receive the desired amount of attention, younger children figure out quite early (sometimes even in the womb!) how to be different from their older siblings. By the way, Casey, who is now a young adult, is a joy to be around and has no problem following the rules (at least that I know of).

KIDS ARE ON A
ROLLER COASTER

*My twelve-year-old son got very mad at me last night
and yelled that he hates me and
that I am the worst mother ever.
Tonight, when I told him I was going to a parenting talk,
he said, "Why? You're the best mom ever!"*
~ Ellen, mother of 3 kids

Kids live on an emotional roller coaster composed of giddy peaks and abysmal valleys: "I'm happy! I'm sad! I'm excited! I'm calm! I love school! I hate school! I love my sister! I hate my sister!" Their moods rise and fall many times every day, sometimes shifting within minutes. Does this sound familiar?

The mistake we make as parents is that we sit right behind them, in the second car of their roller coaster, going along on their ride: "My kid is behaving, I'm a good parent. My kid is misbehaving, I'm a bad parent. My kid is happy, I'm a wonderful parent. My kid is sad, I'm a terrible parent. My kids are getting along, I'm a great parent. My children are arguing, I'm a terrible parent." Up and down we go, mirroring our children's emotions, and allowing them to dictate our mood.

Parents need to be more stable,
not happy one minute and mad the next.
~Tommy, 13 years old

When my kids are miserable, I'm miserable,
and I hate that. If my kids are miserable
when they leave for school, I feel bad all day.
Then they come home, and they're completely fine!
I've spent the day feeling awful,
and they've moved past it.
~Terri, mother of 2 teens

My youngest daughter is more moody.
I tend to pick up on how she's feeling and if she's upset
it gets me going and then I get anxious
and contribute to her anxiety. On the other hand
if she's happy then I tend to be happier.
~Paula, mother of 3 teens

Here's a piece of advice for you: *get off their roller coaster!* You can't stop your kids from riding their roller coaster, *but you don't have to ride it with them.* You should ride your own roller coaster, whose peaks and valleys are dictated by *your* emotions, and whose trajectory is (hopefully) much mellower than your kids'. Riding your own roller coaster, you can stay calm and level-headed while your kids have their big ups and downs. As one mom told me, "My kids can ride the E-ticket rides at Disneyland. I'll enjoy *It's a Small World.*"

It's taken several years of getting it wrong, but we've finally learned to be calm and steady when our children are on a roller coaster. We try to acknowledge their feelings, reassure them that everything will work out or is okay, and also set the limit to how much complaining/crying/whining we'll accept before they need to go to their bedrooms.
~Sierra, mother of 3 kids

Our children need us to be stable. They need to know that we're going to be calmly waiting for them when their roller coaster rolls to a stop. No matter how emotional our kids get, if we stay calm, they will eventually calm down. And as parents, don't we feel better when we stay in control of our emotions?

My mom's reaction depends on her mood.
-Amy, 15 years old

KIDS ACT THEIR WORST WHERE THEY FEEL THE SAFEST

When my kids become wild and unruly,
I use a nice, safe playpen.
When they're finished, I climb out.
~Erma Bombeck, columnist

And where do our kids feel the safest? At home! That's the good news and the bad news. It's the good news because, given the choice, wouldn't you rather your kids misbehave at home rather than at school, at the library, or in the grocery store? It's the bad news because *we're at home with them.* We're the ones who get stuck with their worst behavior.

My youngest doesn't always want to go to gymnastics
She might be tired from a long day of school
and doing homework. She'll whine and complain
about having to go. However, when she gets there
she puts on her "happy" face, gets enthusiastic
and is compliant in front of her coaches.
~Robert, father of 2 teens

This shouldn't surprise us. Where do we adults act our worst? At home, of course. If we're angry at our boss, we just smile politely and say, "I'll get to that tomorrow," as we walk out the door. But then we drive home too fast, slam the front door, kick the dog and yell at the kids. We act our worst at home, because we know that our love and our place in the family is secure despite our bad behavior.

My daughter, just under a year old, already knows how to turn on the shine. She smiles and laughs for people and usually behaves pretty well when we are out. She saves her tantrums for when she's home, mostly when she's getting ready for bed or having her diaper changed.
~Melissa, mother of 1 toddler

Kids know from a young age that it would be wrong to show their worst behavior at school or at a friend's home. They know that there are expectations of their behavior, and they do try to meet those expectations. Often, in exasperation, we say to our kids, "Would you talk that way at your friend's house?" And our kids look at us like we are nuts, and say, "No. Duh. Of course not!" And they probably are right!

Have you ever arrived to pick up your child from day care just to have him burst into tears? The teachers say, "He's been fine all day; we have no idea what's wrong!" Well, your child is crying because five hours earlier, when something bad or sad or scary happened, he didn't feel safe enough to cry. But now, when Dad the Safety Net walks in, he falls apart.

During a "bad" phase with our six-year-old daughter, she would often not get ready in time for school and have fits over socks or clothes not feeling comfortable. Then, she'd be happy and carefree the moment she arrived at school. At the end of the day, she'd be great and happy and silly, but the moment she got in the car she would be rude and grumpy and non-cooperative.
~Andrew, father of 3 kids

But when you're at home with a child who is whining or not listening or complaining about homework, you're probably not thinking, "I'm so happy that my child feels safe!" You're probably feeling like you're the only parents in the world who have a kid who behaves this badly. Wrong! Most children act this way, and you are not alone with this parenting concern.

One day, 14 year old Mark's mother called me and said, "He's misbehaving. He's out of control. He's arguing with us. He's throwing things. He won't listen to a word we say. We can't handle him. Come get him." I immediately jumped in my car, drove to the home of this family in a very difficult situation, and brought him home with me for the weekend.

How did he behave at my house? Beautifully! He was friendly, helpful, and polite. My kids loved him. My husband loved him. Even my dog loved him. He was a pleasure to have around my family, and he posed no behavior challenge for three days.

When I took him home, I talked with his parents. "It's not okay that Mark misbehaves with you," I said. "Together we will come up with a behavioral plan that will improve how he acts at home. But you need to stop calling him a bad kid. He could not come to my house and be polite, friendly, and helpful if he is a bad kid. Mark is a polite, friendly, and helpful teenager who knows that he can get away with misbehaving with his parents."

Mark was out of control at home because his parents did not impose enough external controls at home. But they were doing an excellent job of raising a boy who knew how to be polite, friendly and helpful.

We should not evaluate our child's behavior and character solely by the actions we witness at home. We really need to consider how our kid behaves when she's not at home. Have you ever had your child's friend's mom say, "Your kid is so well behaved"? And you're thinking, "Are you talking about *my* kid? *Your* kid is awesome." Your child acts great at her house, and her kid acts great at your house. That's how it works.

I yell at my mom because she is my mom.
I would never yell at any other parent.
~Emily, 16 years old

Sometimes my young kids would eat dinner with their elbows on the table, slurping their food and chewing loudly. I would say, "Time out. I need proof that you can eat politely. Give me two minutes of polite eating." They would sigh and roll their eyes, but also sit up, pull their elbows off the table, put one hand in their lap, and eat a few bites (chewing with their mouths closed!). After a couple of minutes, I'd say, "Okay, I just needed to see it. You can relax again. I don't mind if you eat like that at home once in a while, but please remember to eat politely everywhere else."

Isn't that really what we want: children who are socially aware enough to know when to use their best manners and their best behavior, and when it's okay to relax a little? Parents get to relax a little at home; so should our children.

KIDS NEED TIME TO BE "BAD": CHOOSING YOUR BATTLES

I've learned to pay attention to my daughter's mood
and my mood, when I'm choosing my battles.
Sometimes we go through good phases;
sometimes we just try to make it through the day.
~Patricia, mother of 1 teen and 1 kid

The wonderful kindergarten teacher of both my children called to share a story. As she always does on the first day of school, she sat her new students down, and explained to them the rules of her classroom. She told them to share, to raise their hands, to be polite, not to run, and so on. She then asked if there were any questions. One little boy raised his hand and asked, "When do we get to be bad?" She and I both laughed with joy at this child's honesty and innocence.

It's okay to break a rule once in a while, to be silly and have fun, to do something different. It's okay to be "bad" once in a while.

All kids are going to be bad sometimes. It's not always fun for us parents when they do, but it's a normal and healthy part of being human. Of course, by "bad" I mean "naughty." Does your kid ever act naughty? Do *you*? Doesn't everyone occasionally misbehave? When your child occasionally misbehaves, instead of worrying that you're a lousy parent, you can smile and think, "Wow, my child is a very normal and healthy human being!"

I want to remind you that it's never the *child* that is bad; it's the *behavior* that is bad. So when we correct our children, we need to be sure that we're making that distinction. We never want to say to our children, "You are bad," because that is what they will then believe about themselves if they hear it often enough. We need to say, "Your *behavior* is not okay," or "Your behavior needs to change." I also like to tell children that they are polite, or friendly or helpful, as opposed to telling them they are "good." All children are good, but I want to praise them for their kindness and their helpfulness.

Now that you know it's normal for your kids to be bad from time to time, here's the best part: as the parent, *you* get to decide what you're going to let them be naughty about. Did you see your daughter jumping on her bed when you walked past her room? You could decide to let her get away with it this time. Did you see your little boy sneak a cookie from the cookie jar? You could choose to cut him some slack this time. Isn't it nice to have a break from constantly pouncing on your kids for their behavior? I'm not advocating allowing your kids to consistently flaunt your family rules, or even break the big ones; I'm giving you permission to sometimes say, "I'm going to pretend I didn't see that."

Our children are allowed to have a tantrum or yell, scream, or do whatever they want to in their rooms. Their bedroom is their haven where they can be as angry as they want to be. They can throw whatever they want and even tear their room apart (they never actually have). They can come out when they are ready to.
~Michael, father of 3 kids

As a parent, you have to choose which battles you're willing to engage in with your kids. When my wonderful daughter got mad, she would stomp to her room and slam the door. The first time she did it, I started down the hallway to her room thinking, "Hey, I'm the mother, and I can't possibly permit that." But then I thought, "Well, I don't really care. She slammed the door. She is expressing her anger. She isn't trashing her room, or hitting me, or breaking possessions. She just slammed her door." And I chose to ignore the behavior at that moment.

I'm not advocating door slamming. I'm not saying you should allow your child to slam the door. I'm telling you that

I made the decision not to confront my daughter for every annoying behavior or action. I'm going to let her be bad sometimes. This is just an example of letting something go because every child—every *person*—misbehaves. We all misbehave from time to time, and we have to let our kids do it, too. I was not comfortable allowing my children to break our values; I was okay if occasionally they broke a minor rule.

Recently, my husband took our daughters to the movies and they saw two movies for the price of one. In other words, they snuck into another theater at the end of the first movie.
~Andrea, mother of 2 teens

A mother of two toddlers called me. "Susan," she asked, "what do I do? They're throwing the ball in the house. I don't know what to do."

I said, "Well, tell them if they throw the ball in the house, you're going to take the ball away."

The next day she called me again. "Susan, what do I do? They're jumping on the couch." This is not an easy one, since we can't take the couch away.

My advice to her was, "Let them. Tell them, 'You're not allowed to jump on the couch at Grandma's house or at the neighbor's house, but here you can jump on the couch.'"

I'm not telling you to allow your kids to jump on your couch, if you think that's wrong. I'm giving you another example of a way to let your kids be bad sometimes. You can't control everything, so you need to decide which battles you're going to engage, and which you're willing to let go— you can't fight them all!

YOUR KIDS WANT YOUR ATTENTION

The quickest way for a parent to get a child's attention is to sit down and look comfortable.
~Lane Olinghouse, author

How many times have you heard "Daddy, watch me, watch me, watch me!" or "Mom, get off the phone!" or "Mom, Dad, come look at this!"? Your kids want your attention all the time. Especially when you are on the phone or in the bathroom. While this constant need for attention can test the limits of a parent's patience, it can also be a useful tool in our parenting toolbox, IF we know how to use it.

Let's look at how we can use our kids' insatiable desire for attention to our advantage.

Give your attention to behaviors you want repeated.

Let's say that we're getting ready to do the dishes, and our two kids start arguing. What do most of us do? We get right there in the middle of it; we're going to get these two kids to knock it off right now. But our kids are smart; they know how things work. They're thinking, "This is great! When we argue, we get Mom and Dad's attention. We can make Mom and Dad stop what they're doing and come in here, just by arguing. It's awesome!" It may be awesome for them, but it's not awesome for us: they get our attention; we get high blood pressure.

Then the next night, when we look into the living room, and our kids are getting along very nicely, we think, "Oh, good. I can go do the dishes in peace," and we tiptoe away without saying anything. This is backwards. We should be giving them our attention when they're behaving the way we'd *like* them to behave, not when they're misbehaving. When we continually pay attention to behaviors we *don't* like, we end up reinforcing bad behavior.

The trick is to start catching your kids acting in ways you like, and then start rewarding their helpful and kind behavior with your attention. When your kids are doing something you like, let them know you appreciate it by giving them some attention. I'm not talking about an hour of praise; just simply say, "Hey, I love the way you guys are cooperating. Thank you."

That's all there is to it: When you see your kids getting along, give them a little attention and then go do the dishes. And when you see your kids arguing, ignore them and go do the dishes. Let them argue. Arguing is a normal part of sibling rivalry.

In elementary school, we had substitute teachers who said, "Boys and girls, everyone who misbehaves will have his or her name written on the board." Billy misbehaved immediately, the substitute put his name on the front board, and everyone spent the next six hours looking at Billy's name. Billy got lots of attention, which is just what he wanted, while the kids who behaved didn't get any.

When I was a substitute teacher, I would say to my students, "Boys and girls, everybody who is polite and helpful will get his or her name on the board." What happened? All day long, students showed me how helpful and polite they could be. I got the behavior I wanted by giving attention to the behavior I wanted.

This works at home, too. Let's say our two kids are sitting at the dinner table and one of them is sitting very nicely and eating politely and the other one is being a total slob. Well, most of us confront the rude one and say, "What are you doing? How many times have I told you put your napkin in your lap? Knock it off!" Meanwhile, the kid who's behaving is thinking, "What do I have to do to get some attention around here?"

Next time this happens at your house, turn to the well-behaved child and say, "Wow, I really appreciate the polite way you're behaving at the dinner table." Give your attention to behaviors that you want repeated. The messy kid will eventually stop misbehaving, in order to get your attention.

Our youngest child would have temper tantrums
and I would have to ignore her
rolling around on the floor crying
and direct all my attention
(it wasn't easy) to the oldest daughter
because she was being kind and good.
~Sarah, mother of 1 toddler and 1 kid

We certainly try to reward the child
with the good behavior, especially with the two boys
2 years apart. They constantly fight over toys, often with
the younger 2-year-old having been the instigator
who takes whatever the 4-year-old wants to play with.
Normally, people would blame the 4-year-old
but we've wised up to the 2-year-old's tricks
and we reward the 4-year-old for tolerating his brother,
and ask the 2-year-old to hand back the toy.
The 2-year-old will be very unhappy and loud about it,
but we try to stick to our guns.
~Greg, father of 2 toddlers

While speaking in classrooms, I keep my eyes on the kids in the back of the room, because I know that the kids who sit back there often misbehave. (Don't ask where I used to sit.) Whenever kids in the back start a conversation with each other, I simply stop talking, and stand quietly. I don't yell at them, or call them out. I just stand there, waiting silently. Soon all the other kids turn around to the misbehaving ones and tell them to be quiet. When the rude kids are quiet again, I continue my talk. I don't reward those misbehaving kids for their rude behavior by giving them my attention.

If you will consistently give your kids attention when they do the right thing, they will do the right thing more often. I guarantee it.

TOEING THE LINE

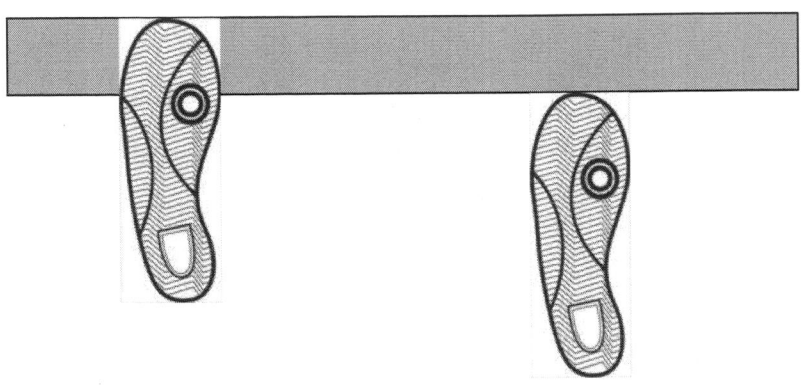

When kids play a running game, or run a race, and they put their foot on a starting line, some kids put their toe on the back of the line, others put their toe on the front of the line, and others will put their toe somewhere in the middle. Which position is correct? In my opinion, all these toe positions are okay, because in all cases, the toe hasn't crossed the line.

Now, let's imagine that this line is our child's behavior. The back of the line is the most preferable behavior, and the front of the line is the very limit of what's acceptable. The area inside the line is our child's wiggle room; it's the behavior that we're willing to let our child get away with.

Let's say that when you tell your daughter, "You need to pick up the clothes that are on the floor of your room," she rolls her eyes, says, "I hate you! You are so mean!" and stomps away to her room. She might even slam the door. How would you feel about these behaviors?

If this were my daughter, responding to my request, I would consider the eye rolling, the "I hate you!" and the stomping to all be behaviors that fall into the wiggle room. In my opinion, as long as she goes to her room and does what I ask, she hasn't crossed the line.

Of course, you may feel differently about this. You may, for instance, feel that eye rolling puts your child across the line. Or, eye rolling may be fine, but saying, "I hate you!" isn't. As parents, we each need to decide which behaviors are in the wiggle room, and which put our kids over the line.

Remember that even if we allow our kids to have some wiggle room, we still need to make sure that there is a limit to what we'll let them get away with, and we need to let our kids know where this outer boundary is. Otherwise, they won't know when to stop.

But having an outer limit isn't always enough. Children are programmed to test their limits, to see where their wiggle room ends. To do this, they will misbehave a little bit, and see if they're stopped. If they're not stopped, they'll misbehave a little more, and see if they're stopped. Kids will keep inching forward until they're stopped by someone in authority. They will push as far as they can, as far as they're allowed. As parents, we need to hold firm on the outer limit, and not worry so much if they roll their eyes and stomp around in the wiggle room.

Don't be afraid to be boss.
Children are constantly testing, attempting to see
how much they can get away with—
how far you will let them go—
and they secretly hope
you will not let them go too far.
~ Ann Landers, advice columnist

PARENT ISSUE OR CHILD ISSUE?

Whenever there's a behavior problem, we have to consider if it's a parent issue or a child issue. Are we causing the problem, or is our child? We need to know who's causing the problem, because it's not fair to be upset with our kid, when it's a parent issue. Often, we might not be causing the problem, but we certainly do contribute to the problem.

Misbehaving, or being a kid?

One hot morning, my teenage son and I were sitting outside a restaurant with several other families, waiting for our table. Among the people waiting was a 9-year-old boy, who was sitting with his family. He was bored; I was bored; everyone was bored. After awhile, the little boy got up, walked over to some pebbles and dirt, and began to play with them. I smiled and thought, "What a great kid! He found something to do. He's not poking his sister, whining, or complaining. He's not throwing the rocks. He's quietly entertaining himself."

Well, the little boy's dad didn't see it that way. He jumped up, grabbed his son, yelled at him to sit down, and shouted, "What are you doing?" This embarrassed everyone in the family. The mom and the grandma stared at the ground, and the sister looked horrified. The little boy started crying. I felt bad for him. In my opinion, he wasn't misbehaving; he was just being a kid.

This family sat quietly until they were finally called to their table. As they filed solemnly into the restaurant, Brandon turned to me and said, "Mom, you would've *told* me to go play in the rocks." He was right! I think kids should be allowed to act like kids.

Let's look at whether this incident was a parent issue or a kid issue. I'm willing to bet that the father felt that his son had ruined the breakfast. In my opinion, I think the dad ruined the breakfast. What do you think? Parent issue, or kid issue?

I once had a mom call me, very upset over what she considered to be a big problem. "We don't know what to do," she said. "Every time we go out to eat, our 4-year-old daughter insists on going to Homestyle Buffet."

I said, "I have an idea. The next time she suggests going to Homestyle Buffet, tell her that you like that restaurant, but tonight it is someone else's turn to choose the restaurant." In other words, simply tell the little girl "No." Since the girl is not paying for the meal or driving the car to the restaurant, then this is a parent issue, not a child issue.

We have to be willing to stop and ask ourselves who is causing the problem, to admit when we are at fault. Everything isn't always our child's fault. We've all been the problem at one time or another. In fact, I think we create a lot of our own problems. I'm a parent; I know. I've been there. I've done it, we've all done it, and we've all witnessed our friends and neighbors and fellow parents at school doing it.

We must change our behavior first.

Insanity: doing the same thing over and over and expecting different results.
~Albert Einstein, scientist

If we want to change our child's behavior, we have to change our behavior first. We can't keep doing the same things over and over again, expecting different results. But as parents, that's often what we do. And it can drive us insane!

Have you ever said to your kids, "How many times do I have to tell you to knock it off?!" Your kids are probably thinking, "I don't know. Ten? Twenty? It doesn't make any difference to me."

We change our behavior when the pain of staying the same becomes greater than the pain of changing.
~Henry Cloud, psychologist and motivational speaker

You can't just keep yelling or grounding your kids or taking away a toy. If what you're doing isn't changing your child's behavior, then you've got to change what you're doing. In other words, if what you're doing isn't working, *try something else!*

THE JOYS OF SIBLING RIVALRY

Take two kids in competition for their parents' love and attention. Add to that the envy that one child feels for the accomplishments of the other; the resentment that each child feels for the privileges of the other; the personal frustrations that they don't dare let out on anyone else but a brother or sister, and it's not hard to understand why in families across the land, the sibling relationship contains enough emotional dynamite to set off rounds of daily explosions.
~Adele Faber, parenting expert and author

Sibling rivalry, the term given for "competitive feelings that naturally occur among children in a family," is the nemesis of many parents. Concerns about sibling rivalry influence many parents' decisions about whether or not to have multiple children: they may carry the physical or psychological scars of their own sibling rivalries, and they may worry about how they will deal with sibling rivalry as parents, or they may just worry how their children will get along.

No matter how calmly you try to referee, parenting will eventually produce bizarre behavior, and I'm not talking about the kids.
~Bill Cosby, comedian and actor

The only way to avoid dealing with sibling rivalry is to have only one child. Otherwise, if you're a parent of two or more children, I guarantee that you will face this concern from time to time.

The relationships between siblings are the most enduring bonds they will have in their lifetimes. We need to allow our kids to build their own connections with their siblings, even if it looks to us as if they're not going to allow each other to reach adulthood.

Dealing with rivalling siblings.

It's normal for children to fight with their siblings from time to time. While sibling fights aren't much fun to witness, they aren't necessarily a sign of a bigger problem or of family dysfunction. Fights don't cause children to grow up hating each other or to end up with twisted psyches. Didn't you fight with your siblings?

Siblings fight because they have to share almost everything: the same Mom and Dad, the same toys, the same pets, the same house, the same food, the same television, the same computer, the same phone, and possibly the same bedroom. They have to share their parents' attention in the form of their time, praise, awards, hugs, and even the size of the cake slice they're given. Siblings who share the same friends may attend the same birthday parties and play dates.

If your kids are just arguing, it's best to let them work it out on their own. In fact, if you run to them every time they yell, you teach them that arguing with their sibling gets your attention. If one child is being hurt, then of course you must intervene immediately, but arguing does not require an immediate parental intervention.

You can help your children to coexist more peacefully if you respect each child's need to be away from his siblings from time to time, and spend one-on-one time with each child. It's also helpful if you don't play favorites among your children or compare them to each other.

You might be tempted to take sides during a sibling dispute, but *don't do it*! You could be fooled by your assumptions about what *really* happened! If you feel that you must intervene when your kids are having a disagreement, listen to both of their stories, and then suggest that they take a break from each other.

Be sure your kids know that it's never okay to hurt their siblings. You might tell your kids, "It's okay to disagree with your siblings or to feel annoyed with them, but I expect you to use your words to resolve things. In our family, it is not okay to hit."

A good thing?

The advantage of growing up with siblings is that you become very good at fractions.
~Robert Brault, author

While sibling rivalry is a fact of life in families with multiple children, it doesn't have to be a problem. In fact, sibling rivalry has benefits—not for the parents, who may end up wondering why they ever thought having more than one child was a good idea—but for the siblings involved.

As they interact with each other, siblings are learning how to share, how to be a friend, how to get along with others, how to be a good winner and a good loser, and how to cooperate.

A disagreement between your children is a great opportunity to teach conflict resolution, negotiation, problem solving and other important life skills. You can start the ball rolling by giving them a choice, such as, "I will give you five minutes to decide which show to watch, but if you can't agree, then the TV will be turned off." Let your kids know that you trust them to resolve the issue themselves.

Now that you have a better understanding of why your children behave they way they do, we'll take a look at how you can calmly and confidently manage their behavior.

Chapter 4

CALM AND COMPETENT BEHAVIOR MANAGEMENT

Children need structure, which includes learning the values of self-discipline and responsibility.
~President Barack Obama

Parenting can be so much fun, and yet so much hard work. Most of us knew this, before we decided to have children. When we embarked on our parenting adventure, we expected to deal with diapers, laundry, car pools, teething, cooking, cleaning, supervising and long-term sleep deprivation, but few of us realized just how difficult and draining it would be, to continually manage our kids' behavior—and our own—all day long, every day. Add to that the our frustration at the perceived or actual lack of cooperation from our kids and our spouses, and parenting can quickly become an ongoing trial by fire.

Parenting would be so much easier if our kids never argued or disagreed with us, if they always cheerfully did everything we wanted them to do, if they always came the first time we called them. But that's not how it usually works. Instead, our kids often butt heads with us, or do things that we don't approve of, or act in ways that we don't like. Situations like these make parenting really tough.

We struggle with behavior management every day. We know that we need to have limits and boundaries, but we don't want to be the bad guy. We want our kids to like us, so we say "Yes" a lot more than we should. We don't want to sound like our parents, so we don't say "No" enough. We think our children are so wonderful and special (which they are), that they should be allowed to do whatever they want (which they aren't).

As much as we'd like to, we can't be our kids' friends. What they really need is for us to be their parents. They have enough friends, but only one Mom and Dad. Children need to be taught how to behave in every situation; they need discipline. And whether we like it or not, as their parents, it's our job to discipline them. According to Dictionary.com, discipline means "training to act in accordance with rules." In other words, to discipline means "to teach."

By disciplining our children, we are teaching them how to behave.

By using my **Three Steps of Behavior Management**, you can gain control of any situation and calmly and competently respond to every behavioral challenge. And one of the best features about the Three Steps—besides their simplicity—is that it doesn't matter whether you're dealing with a toddler, a kid, or a teen: the Three Steps work beautifully with any age group.

Ready to take control? Ready for more cooperation and less conflict? Here, then, are my **Three Steps of Behavior Management.**

STEP ONE: ESTABLISH YOUR FAMILY RULES

Our rules are no hitting to solve problems,
and be careful with other people's stuff or ask first.
~Julia, 6 years old

Rules make children feel safe and secure, even if they do not like them. Rules let kids know what is expected of them and what they can and cannot do. Rules teach our children that they are not in control of every situation and that their society has rules about behavior.

Remember when you tightly swaddled your infant with a soft blanket so she felt secure and protected? Flailing arms and legs make infants feel unsafe; being held tightly makes them feel safe. Well, now that they're older, we need to swaddle our kids with rules. The first step in this process is to establish a List of Family Rules. Be sure to call them "family rules." They're not *the* rules, they're *our* rules. I often ask parents what their rules are and many have a hard time answering. But the truth is that every family has rules, and every parent and child should know their family rules. It's much easier to follow the rules if you know what they are.

Family rules can include, "Wash your hands before you eat," "No swearing," or "Use your indoor voice." Parents often ask me what their rules should be, but I can't answer that. Family rules are based on personal values, and should reflect how you want your children to live their lives, and how you are living yours.

My husband and I took three-year-old Brandon to a restaurant with friends who had a daughter a few months younger. We shared a booth, with each family sitting on one side. Brandon asked if he could stand up, and I told him,

"Yes, as long as you don't turn around and bother the people behind us."

The little girl immediately asked if she could stand up, and her parents said, "No, we don't do that in restaurants." When she pouted, they said, "Here, have a sip of Daddy's beer."

As we drove home, I said to my husband, "Can you believe that they allowed her to have a sip of beer?"

And I'm sure that our friends drove home saying, "Can you believe that they allowed him to stand up?"

Their rule: No standing up in the booth. Our rule: No alcohol for children. Every family has different values and different rules, and it's important that everyone in the family knows and understands what they are.

The main themes of our family rules are:
1) Mom and Dad are in charge.
2) We are nice and kind to others and each other.
3) We are a safe and healthy family.
4) We cooperate and work together as a family.
5) We try our best.
~Thomas, father of 3 kids

Establishing family rules can save you from lengthy discussions with your children about why they can or cannot do something. How many times do we hear, "But everyone else can do it?" or "Why can't I?"

Ten-year-old Casey came home and asked if she could have a TV in her room. When I told her she couldn't, she said, "But Emily has a TV in *her* room."

I didn't say what I wanted to say, which was, "Emily's parents are wrong." I just said, "That's okay, but in *our* family, children don't get televisions in their rooms. It's one of our family rules." End of discussion.

I don't let the cat out if she's not supposed to go out.
I keep the nebulizer on my face until it's done.
~ Alison, 3 years old

My rules are no back talking, no hitting,
and no hurting each other.
~Craig, 11 years old

My rule is to be nice.
~Amy, 8 years old

Here are the rules.
No climbing on top of the roof of the play structure.
No climbing the palm tree.
No climbing on the roof of our house.
No taking thorns off the rosebushes to make a knife.
No sharpening our kitchen knives.
We're not allowed to climb on the top
of the basketball hoop.
No lighting candles without permission.
~ Pete, 8 years old

I have to listen to Mom & Dad.
Do your jobs.
Don't break the slide anymore with rocks.
No hitting, kicking, or punching.
~Jason, 7 years old

My rules are: turn off phone on time, go to school
every day, and make sure to go to bed on time.
~Debbie, 15 years old

Most of our rules center on respect for each other.
~Bridget, mother of 2 kids and 1 teen

*Kids need to stay in the house or yard
unless they're with a grown-up. No hitting.*
~Renee, mother of 1 toddler and 1 kid

*We don't eat in the living room, we share our toys,
we are nice to one another, we use our manners.
No yelling (Mommy breaks this one sometimes).
No hitting one another, yet we sometimes
spank our children.*
~Roger, father of 2 kids

*Our rules include: listening to and respecting others,
being honest, doing homework, no TV or media during
play dates, eating healthy food before treats,
being kind and using good communication skills.*
~Mark, father of 1 toddler and 1 kid

*Speak respectfully to each other. Help each other.
If rules are broken, we count to 3 and have the
consequence attached. We have taken away screen time
but again, have not had to do much because the
boundaries are set and he knows we follow through.
Tonight he said, "Please don't get to 3, Daddy."*
~Rebecca, mother of 1 kid

Always tell the truth or own up to something
you have done wrong. Keep grades up to the best of
your ability. Do unto others as you would have
them do unto you. Trust, school, and
trying to be a good person are important.
~Wanda, mother of 2 teens

Live honorably, with integrity.
Be honest and respectful of others.
Keep the house clean, or get nagged.
Do homework promptly. Always do your best.
~Ben, father of 2 teens

If we expect our kids to follow the rules, they've got to know what the rules are. If I walked into almost any classroom, I'd see a posted list of classroom rules. Teachers post the rules for two reasons. The first is to remind students what's expected of them, so the kids can't say, "We didn't know it was a rule." The other reason is to save the teachers from having to yell. They can quite calmly say, "Wait a minute. That's rule number four. It's been posted here from the first day of class. You know that's not okay."

It's a good idea to post your family rules. Now, you might be thinking, "We have 89 rules. I can't possibly post all 89 rules!" You're right; your fridge isn't big enough. Just post your Top Five rules. How do you decide what your Top Five rules are? Your Top Five rules relate to whatever behaviors your kids are doing right now that annoy you, whatever rules your kids are consistently breaking, whatever behaviors you're having challenges with.

Let's say you notice that one of your kids is swearing. Time for a new family rule! Let your kids know there's a new family rule—No Swearing—and post it where they can see it. Now, when your child swears and then claims he didn't know swearing was against the rules, you can calmly direct his attention to the posted list of family rules, where it clearly says, No Swearing.

Rules should be clear and measurable. Marie, a mother of two young children, said that when she was young, her mother would say, "Be home before dark." Marie and her sister remembered the rule, and always tried to get home before dark. But when they got home, their mom would often be upset and tell them they were late; that it was already dark. Marie and her sister didn't break the rule; they simply had a different idea of "dark." A better rule would be, "Be home by 5:30." That is a clear and measurable rule.

The same goes for when we tell our kids, "Clean your room." I guarantee that you and your child each have a different idea of what "clean" is. A more clear direction is, "Put away all your clothes, pick everything up off your floor, and close all your dresser drawers." *That* is a clear and measurable direction.

STEP TWO: DETERMINE CONSEQUENCES

If I break a rule , I get in trouble.
~ Maggie, age 8

Every rule should include a corresponding set of positive and negative consequences. If your kids follow a rule, they get a positive consequence; if they break a rule, they get a negative consequence.

Let's say, for instance, that you have a family rule that all homework must be done before the TV goes on. What are some positive consequences for following this rule? The TV can go on, Mom and Dad are pleased, and your homework is all done. What might be some negative consequences, if you disregarded the rule and turned the TV on before your homework was finished? Now, your parents are angry because you were dishonest and sneaky, your homework isn't done, and you're not allowed to watch TV the next day. Every rule needs to have both positive and negative consequences.

Having pre-determined consequences for your family rules will help you to remain calm and in control when your child breaks a rule, because you will already know how to handle that situation.

Positive consequences.

Positive consequences can be either *extrinsic* or *intrinsic* rewards. An extrinsic reward is something physical that your child receives for following a rule. Examples of extrinsic rewards are stickers, candy or money.

We might choose to give our child an extrinsic reward if she's achieved something that she's been struggling with, or that's new or hard to do. Potty training is one example where parents often use extrinsic rewards. Or, we might have a kid who's having a hard time getting his homework done. In that case, for a brief period, we might tell him, "Every time you get your homework done and turned in, you get a sticker."

Extrinsic rewards should be given sparingly. Don't get into the habit of giving your kids an extrinsic reward every time they do the right thing. Your kids should do the right thing because they know you *expect* them to do the right thing, not because they're looking to get something.

A better kind of positive consequence is an intrinsic, or internal, reward. Examples of intrinsic rewards are praise, a smile, a hug or not having Mom or Dad yell. I'm not talking about going overboard with praise, but if your child follows a rule, just say, "Thanks!" and let that be enough.

> *My generation was raised to expect a trophy*
> *every time we got out of bed in the morning.*
> ~Aaron, 26 years old

We want our kids to understand that it feels good to do the right thing. We want them to know that when they do the right thing, good things happen, and when they do the wrong thing, then bad things can happen.

Negative consequences.

Let's say that you've chosen your family rules. You've discussed them. You've posted them. You've made sure your kids know them. Now you have to determine the consequence for breaking a rule. There's no point in having a rule, if there's no negative consequence for breaking it.

If we break the rules in our house
my little sister has a time out for three minutes
and my dad tells me not to do it.
~ Mark, 8 years old

When you break a rule,
then you stay in your time out
and say sorry to people when you're done.
~Benny, 4 years old

My mom counts to 5 and then I go to my room.
But I can play in there and so it's okay.
~Spencer, 4 years old

Consequences at my house are
no screens for one week, and no TV and computer.
~Stephen, 11 years old

If I break a rule, I lose TV and computer privileges
and have to go to my room for a time-out.
~Lori, 8 years old

At my house, if you break a rule, you have to go to your room for two minutes until you calm down.
~Vincent, 6 years old

If I don't follow the rules, my phone gets taken away, I get grounded and have no social privileges until I can prove myself.
~ Beth, 16 years old

We usually institute a time out in their room, a few moments to collect themselves and come back to the situation.
~Wendy, mother of 2 toddlers

If rules are broken the older one is given a time-out and the younger one is just reminded of the rule.
~Brian, father of 1 toddler and 1 kid

When it seems family members are forgetting our family rules too often, we in theory get out the rules and review them.
~Ariana, mother of 3 kids

We try to give consequences for breaking family rules, but sometimes we end up yelling and giving time outs.
~Emily, mother of 1 toddler and 1 kid

When rules are broken, we usually end up doing time outs and making apologies, although a lot of the apologies are insincere, so I don't know how useful that is.
~Lena, mother of 1 toddler and 2 kids

It's nice when the negative consequence matches the misdeed. Lots of parenting books and experts say, "Make sure the consequence matches the misbehavior." This is a great idea, but in the nitty-gritty of daily parenting, it's hard to always come up with a consequence that aligns perfectly with the offense. And that's okay.

If your child breaks a rule for which you don't already have a pre-determined consequence, it's perfectly reasonable to tell your child, "Go to your room for ten minutes," as a consequence. What's important is that your child receives a negative consequence for breaking a rule. It's much better to provide a general consequence at the time, than to hesitate, trying to think up the perfect consequence for the situation, while the opportunity for the lesson slips away.

STEP THREE: FOLLOW THROUGH

Enforcing consequences is always hard. It kills me.
But I know that if I don't follow through,
I'm teaching my kids that they can negotiate
their way out of it.
~Anita, mother of 3 kids

This is without a doubt the hardest step, where parents sometimes lose their resolve. But it's also the *most important step*, where the lesson is taught. Once you've made the rules, determined the consequences, and discussed them with your kids, you *must* follow through with whatever consequences your child expects from breaking a rule. Don't set up a consequence that you're not sure you'll be able to enforce. Make sure you choose a consequence that you're going to follow through with, so your kids will know what will happen when they get caught breaking a rule.

There are two great injustices that can befall a child.
One is to punish him for something he didn't do.
The other is to let him get away with doing something
he knows is wrong.
~Robert Gardner, filmmaker and author

Kids are smart; they know if their parents are likely to let them sidestep consequences. You don't want your kids to think, "I won't get caught," or "I can do it because Dad threatens me with things all the time, and he never does it." It's really important that your kids believe that you will do what you say.

Sometimes my mom doesn't
follow through with consequences.
Instead, she nags my brother and me,
to try to make us do what we're supposed to do.
I don't like it when my mom nags.
I wish she would just go full force
and do what she said she was going to do.
~Rachel, 13 years old

Following Through is the hardest of the Three Steps, but here's another way to think about it that might make it easier for you: Your child *chose* to break the rule, knowing what the consequence would be. By following through, you're just *supporting his choice*. It's not *your* fault that he can't watch television. It's not *your* fault that he can't go out tonight. It's your *child's* fault.

Saying, "This was your choice," makes me feel
a little better, when I have to follow through
with a consequence.
~Patricia, mother of 2 kids

When we drive on the freeway, we see speed limit signs posted at regular intervals. We all know that the speed limit on highways is 65 miles an hour. We also know what the negative consequences are for breaking this law: It's going to cost me money. It's going to cost me time. It's going to be embarrassing. I'll have to go to traffic school. We know what the consequences are.

Then why do so many people speed? Two reasons: either they don't mind the consequences or they think they won't get caught. This is because most of the time, they *do* get away with it. Most of the time, there's no follow-through. If every time somebody sped, they got a ticket, they would choose not to speed. They would do the right thing.

That's why you need to follow through with consequences. You don't want to raise children who think they can get away with things. You want to raise children who know that if they break a rule, they will be caught, and they will have to face the consequences. The way to do this is to consistently enforce your family rules by following through with the consequences.

Not following through is lying.

I went to observe a six-year-old boy who struggles with ADHD and whose parents were looking for help in managing his behavior. While I was in their home, the boy became frustrated and threw a toy. His mother said, "If you do that one more time, I am going to take your Wii away from you."

The boy immediately replied with a loud and firm, "You liar!" His parents gasped—as do most parents when I share this story—and turned to me for help. Instead of reprimanding the boy for his rudeness, I asked him why he'd said that. "Because she always tells me that, and she never does it," he said.

I turned back to the mom and said, "I agree with your son. You are a liar."

By not following through with their stated consequences, these parents are teaching their son that he doesn't have to listen to them because nothing bad happens when he doesn't listen. They're teaching him that it's okay to tell someone you will do something, and then not do it. And they're teaching him that because they sometimes lie, he should question everything they say.

Telling their son that they would take a toy away as a consequence for a naughty behavior is totally appropriate. They gave him a direction and a consequence, which is good parenting. But without any follow through, there is no consequence. And without a consequence, there really is no rule.

Let's say that you tell your child, "If you watch TV before your homework is done, you won't be allowed to watch TV tomorrow," and then you catch your child watching TV before her homework is done. Of course, being a good parent, you will enforce the consequence and your daughter won't be allowed to watch TV the next day. Right?

But if you *don't* enforce the negative consequence, if you allow your child to watch TV, after you told her that you wouldn't, you have not only neglected to follow through; you have also *lied* to your child. You told your child you would do something, and then you didn't do it. That's lying.

Remember earlier, when we talked about how to raise an honest adult? We said that to raise an honest adult, we need to *be* an honest adult. Well, when we don't follow through with something that we told our children, we're not being honest. If we're going to be the person we want our kids to be, we can't lie to them. Our kids need to know that they can rely on us to do what we say we'll do.

Your kids probably won't think, "She's a liar," if you don't follow through with consequences. But they might think, "She's a flake," or "She'll let me get away with anything." You don't want your children to grow up thinking, "I can't trust my parents." If your kids grow up thinking, "I don't believe everything my parents say, because sometimes they mean it and sometimes they don't," then, when you say things like, "I love you," "I like you," "I'm proud of you," or "I want to spend time with you," they've got that little voice whispering, "My parents don't always mean what they say, so I'm not totally convinced that they mean it."

We all want our kids to believe us. Part of that is having them believe that if they break a rule, they will receive the negative consequence. The flip side is that when we tell them we are proud of them, they'll know we mean it.

If you as parents cut corners, your children will, too.
If you lie, they will, too.
~Marian Wright Edelman, founder, Children's Defense Fund

Another side of honesty is admitting—and then correcting —our mistakes. We can't say we're going to impose a consequence, if we're not going to enforce it. Of course, every once in a while, we'll get frustrated and blurt out something like, "No television for a month!" It's okay to go back later and say, "You know what? I was feeling really frustrated when I said no television for a month. That's silly. I know I'm not going to stick to that. I should've said, 'No television for two days,' because that's a more realistic consequence; so it's going to be no TV for two days."

That's not letting our kids off the hook; it's owning up to our mistake. Successful adults admit their mistakes. Successful adults step up and say, "I said something wrong. I blurted it out in frustration." You can go back and fix it. It's okay.

THE THREE STEPS WORK IN ANY SITUATION

It's great when our kids break a rule that's on our family rule list because we feel prepared to handle it. There's the rule, there's the consequence. End of story. But the challenge of parenting is the hundred times a day when we tell our child to do something and they don't do it. "Pick it up," "put it down," "put it on," "take it off"...you know how it goes. What do we do when our child breaks a rule that's not on our list of family rules?

One day, I was riding in the car with my friend and her children, when her son began to kick his mother's seat. My friend said, "Hey, knock it off!" When the boy did it again, my friend got louder, "I told you to knock it off!" And when her son did it yet again, my friend turned around and yelled, "How many times do I have to tell you not to kick my seat!?"

You just know the boy was thinking, "I don't know, thirty? As many times as you want." My friend felt out of control, and her son knew it. In fact, it was kind of funny to him. His mother's face was getting redder and redder, and her voice was getting higher and higher. She was starting to perspire. Her son thought it was funny, watching his mother get so upset. Eventually, my friend pulled over, turned around, screamed at her son and threatened to keep him home from a party on the weekend. Then, he stopped kicking her seat.

When our kids break one of our posted rules, we know exactly how to handle it, because we already know what the consequence is, and we can just follow through with it. But what should we do, when our children misbehave in ways that aren't covered by a posted rule? How do we handle these situations effectively?

The answer is simple: we use the Three Steps.

Let's replay the seat-kicking scene, with the mother using the Three Steps—Establishing a Rule, Determining a Consequence, and Following Through—instead of yelling and getting frustrated.

We're riding in the car and my friend's son kicks her seat. My friend looks at her son in the rear view mirror and says, "Hey, Honey, please don't kick my seat. I find it really distracting when I'm driving. I need to focus on the road, and when you kick my seat, it distracts me, and it's not safe." By speaking calmly to her son, the mother did two positive things: she explained to her child *why* she didn't like it, and *why* it's unsafe, which is important information; and she left open the possibility that he didn't kick her seat on purpose. Maybe he'd swung his leg, and kicked her seat by accident. Kids aren't always misbehaving. It's okay to give them the benefit of the doubt sometimes.

When my friend's son kicks her seat the second time, she's pretty sure that it wasn't an accident. Now, she looks at her son in the rear view mirror and says, "I've asked you to stop kicking my seat." There's the Rule. "If you kick my seat one more time, I'm pulling the car over to the side of the road, and we're going to sit for five minutes." There's the Consequence.

Now, it's up to her son to decide whether he wants to experience the positive consequence—getting to his destination on time—or the negative consequence—having to wait in the car and possibly be late. If he decides to kick his mother's seat again, she *must* pull off the road for five minutes. There's the Follow-through.

By using the Three Steps—responding to her son's seat kicking with a Rule, a Consequence, and a Follow-through— my friend was able to take control of what could have become a dangerous and frustrating situation and bring it to a calm resolution.

Any time your kids are doing something you don't like, even if it's not one of your established rules, you can use the Three Steps. Every time you tell your child to do something, think of that as Step One: Setting a Rule. Then, if she doesn't act on your request, you can move down the list of the Steps as far as you need to. You can say, "This is the rule, and this is what's going to happen if you choose to ignore the rule." Then, it's up to your child to decide which she prefers.

Here's another example of using the Three Steps on the fly: While I was babysitting Samantha, an adorable seven-year-old, she placed her equally adorable puppy on her lap during dinner. I told Samantha to put the puppy down (there's the Rule) and explained that it was unfair to tease the puppy with food. Samantha sighed deeply, rolled her eyes, and said, "You are not my mother and you can't make me."

I agreed with her, and then said, "If you choose to keep the puppy on your lap, then I will take your dinner plate away" (there's the Consequence). After a couple moments of consideration and a few more sighs, Sam put the puppy down and I thanked her for making a good choice. I was prepared to Follow Through, and Sam knew that.

Ask, Tell, Provide a Consequence.

A modified version of the Three Steps, that we can use when we ask a child to do something and he doesn't comply, is what I call the **Ask, Tell, Provide a Consequence Method**. Here's how it works: Let's say that my child is watching television in the family room when it's time for dinner. I first **Ask** my child to come to the dinner table: "Brandon, please come to dinner."

If he doesn't come, I walk closer to him and **Tell** him in a louder voice, "It's time for dinner. Come to the table."

If he still doesn't come, I **Provide a Consequence**: "It's time to come to the table. If you're not at the table in five minutes, you will not have dinner tonight" (insert your own consequence here). Then, depending on whether my child comes to dinner or not, I will either have a nice dinner with him, or I will follow through with the consequence and eat dinner without him.

The specific consequence isn't what matters. What matters is not having to argue with our child, not having to tell our child the same thing ten times, getting louder each time, and eventually shrieking at him to come to the table in our loud screechy voice.

Here is an example of a situation when I used the **Ask, Tell, Provide a Consequence Method** of behavior modification:

While I was babysitting Alexis, an exuberant 26-month-old, she threw a toy at me. I asked her not to throw the toy at me again. When she threw it at me the second time, I told her, "If you choose to throw the toy again, I will take it away and you will not be able to play with it again today." Alexis threw the toy again, and so I promptly put the toy on the top shelf and told her that she could have it back the next day, and hopefully she would choose not to throw it again.

The **Three Steps of Behavior Management** truly can be used in any situation, and they really work.

FIRST THIS—AND THEN THAT

I want to introduce you to what I call the **First This— And Then That** method of behavior management. The basic idea is that you tell your child what he needs to do **first**, and **then** what he can do after he's done what you asked.

When your child is two years old, it looks like this: "First you put your dirty spoon on the counter, and then we can play."

In elementary school, it looks like this: "First you do your homework, and then you can use the computer."

In middle and high school, it looks like this: "First you earn my trust, and then I'll give you some independence."

Now that you know these effective methods to manage your child's behavior, you'll be able to calmly handle any behavior situation with confidence and style. Other parents will be amazed by your simple yet effective techniques for managing your child's behavior!

Because the Three Steps rely on your child's *choices* about which consequences she will receive for her actions, we'll spend some time in the next chapter, discussing how you can teach your child to make good choices.

Chapter 5

ALLOW YOUR CHILD TO MAKE CHOICES

My boys make a lot of choices—
after all, that's what builds character and independence.
I remind them that messing up is part of learning.
We have to pick ourselves up, dust ourselves off,
and move on.
~Adriana, mother of 2 kids and 1 teen

One warm August morning, when four-year-old Sam arrived at my home-based nursery school, he was wearing winter boots, a parka and a Spiderman cape. When I saw him, I just had to laugh.

His mother shrugged and said, "I didn't pick out his outfit."

I said, "No, really?"

Within one hour, Sam was running around barefoot and his cape was gone. When Sam went home, I asked him what he was going to wear the next day. He replied, "My flip-flops and my shorts." Sam had learned a valuable lesson all by himself, and would make a better choice the next day.

I thought it was great that Sam's mom let him pick out his clothes. It was a perfect opportunity for Sam to practice making choices: this choice wasn't going to get him hurt or into trouble, or keep him from getting into college. But it would allow him to exercise his decision-making skills, which would serve him well throughout his life.

If you take away only one word from reading this book, I would want that word to be CHOICE. Everything that your kids do is a choice. Everything we adults do is a choice. Every movement we make, every word we say, is a choice. This, to me, is the Number 1 trait of being a successful adult: understanding that everything we do is a choice, that every choice has consequences, and that we need to make good choices.

The adult brain is not fully developed until our mid-twenties, and the last part to develop helps us make good decisions. But we cannot wait for our kids to be adults before we expect them to make good choices. We need to teach them how to make good choices, long before they need to do it by themselves, and from as young an age as possible. Even toddlers can be given some simple choices to make.

The **Three Steps of Behavior Management**—Setting Rules, Determining Consequences and Following Through—that we learned about in the previous chapter, are effective because we allow our *child* to choose whether she would rather experience the positive consequences of following the rule, or the negative consequences of breaking the rule. It's her choice. And that makes all the difference.

> *It's really annoying, how my parents make*
> *all my decisions for me. They do that because*
> *they think I can't do it myself,*
> *even though I know I can.*
> ~Penny, 14 years old

A mom told me that her family has a rule against hitting. The consequence for hitting is that whoever hits doesn't get dessert that evening. One day, her ten-year-old son, Nicky, was punching his younger brother and the mom said, "Nicky, if you hit your brother one more time, you're not getting dessert."

Nicky stopped and looked up at his mother, his arm still cocked and asked, "What are we having?"

SUCCESSFUL ADULTS
MAKE GOOD CHOICES

Children must be allowed to make decisions for themselves, if they're going to grow up into successful adults. As parents, we get to decide how many and what kinds of choices our child can make, based on her age and how much we trust her. Even if the choices seem small and unimportant, we have to begin to let our kids make their own decisions. We don't want our children to grow up depending on us to make all their choices for them.

We allow our daughter to make her own choices and be responsible for her actions.
~Tom, father of 1 teen

Our youngest son wants to make his own choices in his sport of diving. He has told us to allow him to direct his diving career with his coach and to not interfere with the decisions made.
~Roger, father of 2 teens

My son is a good money saver
and I allowed him to spend his money on a computer.
He did all the research into finding the right computer
that he could afford. It was a good lesson, because
he learned about all the hidden costs.
~Brian, father of 1 kid and 1 teen

My younger son is deciding not to
complete his last year in Little League.
I'm trying to be supportive even though
I would like him to play one more year.
~Patricia, mother of 2 teens

START EARLY

If you don't give your kid freedom to make choices
with money, including stupid choices,
he'll make plenty when he gets to college.
~John Gardner, author

Even though they're little, we can start allowing our children to make choices when they're toddlers. We can ask our two-year-old, "Do you want a waffle or cereal for breakfast?" or, "Do you want to put on your shirt first or your socks first?" This will get him used to the idea of choosing.

Cake is not healthy.
But you can eat it after you eat the healthy food.
~Diane, 4 years old

Allowing a child to make choices does not mean that the child always gets to decide what to do. Let's say that your toddler has just eaten a bowl of spaghetti and has sauce all over his face. You try to wipe his face, but he will not hold still. Ask him, "Do you want to wipe your face or should I?" In other words, whether or not to have his face wiped is not a choice. *How* it gets wiped is a choice.

It's important that our toddler learns to make choices because when he grows into a teenager, he will be making many choices—some of which will be important, and may be potentially life-altering—that we may never know about: "Should I cut school? Should I smoke pot? Should I drink? Should I smoke a cigarette? Should I sneak around and not tell my parents?" We're not there when our teen is making these choices, so we want to make sure that he has been making choices for himself since he was a toddler, so he'll know how to do it well.

MAKING A CHOICE MEANS CHOOSING THE CONSEQUENCE

When we allow our kids to make their own decisions, we must also allow them to reap (or suffer) the consequences. Everything they do is a choice and every choice has a consequence. That just goes with the territory.

We can remind our children of the possible consequences of a choice, but then we need to step back and allow them to make the decision. Sometimes that's really hard, especially when we see our kids making a choice that we wouldn't have made. But that's the whole point of letting our kids make some of their own decisions! That's where their confidence is created and lessons are learned.

We need to let our kids make their own decisions and then no matter how much we want to run in and rescue them, we don't do it! Our goal is to raise a successful adult, who can make choices and deal with the consequences. We're not going to accomplish that if we rescue our kids all the time. They have to deal with the consequences of their decisions. And we have to let them.

Usually, I offer my girls two or three choices
that are acceptable to me.
~Mark, father of 1 toddler and 1 kid

My kids choose their own clothing,help plan meals,
choose how to spend their allowance (with some
guidelines), and choose TV shows (also with some
guidelines). They spend their free time doing anything
they choose as long as it is safe and they clean up
when they are done.
~Anne, mother of 2 kids

We allow our kids to choose their clothes.
We start the process the night before, because they are
usually in good spirits and it helps in the morning rush.
We let them choose snack options, drink options,
activities that the family participates in, and
shows that they watch.
~Chris, father of 2 kids

We try to give him lots of choices such as when he wants
to play, clean up, bathe, etc. He has boundaries but
within what we need to happen, we allow choices.
~Deirdre, mother of 1 kid

EVERYTHING IS A CHOICE

One time, while speaking to a group of high school students, I told them, "Everything you do is a choice."

One teen raised his hand and said, "Uh-uh, we didn't have a choice. We *had* to come here today."

So I walked over to him and looked all around his chair. "Where are your chains?" I asked.

"What?"

"You said you had to come here today, so I want to see the chains that must be holding you in that chair."

"I just meant I would have gotten in trouble if I hadn't come," he said.

"Well then, good for you," I said, "You *did* have a choice, and you made the right choice. You considered your options and made the decision to come and not get in trouble even though you didn't want to."

You know your own kids. I can't tell you which decisions to allow them to make and which ones you're going to have continue to make for them. Perhaps you'll let your five-year-old son decide what shirt he wears to Grandma's house, but you won't let him decide how many cookies to eat for a snack before dinner. Perhaps you'll let your teenage daughter decide how long she works on her history report, but you won't let her decide whether to skip the SAT and go shopping with friends, instead.

We allow our kids to make their own choices about tons of things, whenever possible.
~Hailey, mother of 4 kids

Once, when I was working with a 15-year-old boy and his parents, the parents called me because the boy had hit his mom. My advice for the parents was this: "The next time your son lays his hands on you in anger, you dial 9-1-1. That's the rule, and that's the consequence."

They said, "We can't tell our son that because we're afraid he'll get mad and hit us again."

I said, "Bring him over to my house, and I'll tell him."

The boy came over to my house the next night, and I said, "Here's the new rule in your house: If you ever lay your hands on your mother again, in anger, your parents are calling 9-1-1."

He said, "Really?"

I said, "Yeah, that's the new rule in your house. But dude, don't hit your mother, and then they won't call 9-1-1. This is totally in your control. This is totally your choice. You know what the rule is, and you know what the consequence is, so choose to do the right thing."

We're in the midst of college applications and
we've allowed our son to choose his campuses
without a whole lot of input from us.
He's done the applications
pretty much on his own,
with occasional reminders from us
about deadlines and follow-up.
~Tom, father of 2 teens

Parents have the responsibility of making the right choice, too. The dad we learned about in Chapter 3, who was so upset with his son for playing in the dirt outside the restaurant, could have made a different choice. He could have chosen to leave his son alone, to allow him this one time to get his hands dirty and to say something later, if needed. He could have chosen to smile and let it go, but he chose, instead, to make a scene and upset his entire family. Everything we do is a choice.

WHAT'S THE WORST THAT CAN HAPPEN?

Has your child ever refused to put on a jacket? Welcome to the club. Most parents have had the pleasure of dealing with his particular situation. My guess is that the conversation probably went something like this:

You, holding your child's jacket out so he can take it: "You need to wear your jacket this morning."

Child: "I don't wanna wear a jacket!"

You: "But it's cold and rainy. You *need* to wear a jacket to school."

Child, folding arms: "I'm *not* gonna wear a jacket."

You, holding the jacket closer to your child: "You're *going* to wear this jacket."

The conversation probably went downhill from there, ending with both of you angry and at least one of you in tears. If you forced your child to wear the jacket, he probably took it off the moment he was out of your sight, anyway.

This scenario is a perfect example of an opportunity for you as a parent to allow your child to make a decision and learn from the consequences. As a parent, it's not your job to force your kid to wear a jacket. But it *is* your job is to help him make a choice, to help him look at his options. Your job as a parent is to have a conversation with your child that goes something like this:

You: "If you choose not to wear a jacket, what might happen?"

Child: "I might be cold."

You: "Anything else?"

Child: "I might be wet."

You: "That's right. You might be uncomfortable. Keep in mind that you're not going to be able to come home early from school. If you get wet, you're going to sit in class all wet. Now, what will happen if you choose to wear your jacket?"

Child: "I would not be cold and I would not be wet."

You: "That's true.

Child: "And I I could take my jacket off, if I'm too hot.

You: "Okay, you know the choices and the consequences. Now, what do you want to do?"

Your child might choose to wear his jacket, or he might cross his arms and say, "I'm *not* wearing my jacket."

Whatever he chooses, you say, "Okay, that's your choice," and *let him do it.*

Should you allow your child to make **all** his own choices? Of course not! Then how do you decide which choices you'll allow your child to make? Here's the trick: ask yourself, *"What's the worst that could happen?"* Then, you have to decide whether you can accept the worst possible consequences of your child's decision. If you can, then you let your child make the choice. If not, then you don't allow him to make the choice. It's that simple.

Let's apply this test to the jacket situation above. Ask yourself, what's the worst that could happen if your son doesn't wear his jacket to school today? He might be wet. He might be cold. He might be uncomfortable. Can you live with those outcomes? Sure! You'll be warm and dry, because you were wise enough to wear your jacket. So you let him choose. And guess what? Your kid is smart. The next day, he'll either wear his jacket if he was uncomfortable enough, or he'll choose not to, because he doesn't mind being wet and cold. It's not such a big deal, and it's good practice, for when kids get the opportunity to make their own choices about bigger issues.

Let's say your child comes up to you with one sentence written on a piece of paper, and says, "I'm not doing any more of this homework."

You say, "But the assignment says to write a paragraph and you only wrote one sentence."

Your kid says, "I don't care! It's stupid and it's boring! I'm not doing any more and you can't make me!"

First ask yourself, "What's the worst that can happen?" If you're okay with the answer, then you say, "You're right. I can't make you do it. But let's look at the possible consequences: What will happen if you finish the assignment? What will happen at school and at home if you don't?" Point out that at school your child might have to skip recess or receive a low grade. Remind her that she may not watch TV until her homework is done. And then you let her decide, trusting that she will learn from her choice.

WE LEARN BY MAKING MISTAKES

Good decisions come from experience,
and experience comes from bad decisions.
~Author Unknown

We all want to raise children who make good choices. It's important to remember that making a "good" choice doesn't mean always making the choice we hope they make. Sometimes, it means making the wrong choice, because that's how we learn. Making bad choices teaches us resiliency and builds our self-confidence.

Sometimes you have to let your kids make bad choices,
as long as the mistake is relatively small.
And sometimes it turns out that you were wrong
and they were right.
~Stephanie, mother of 2 teens

My parents monitor everything I do. My dad says that he
tells me what to do all the time because he wishes that
someone had told him what to do, when he was young.
I tell him, "Yeah, but you got to learn from what you did.
How can I learn, if you don't let me make choices?"
~Beth, 13 years old

Years ago, before digital cameras, my eight-year-old neighbor, Jonathan, was sharing the pictures he took on a family vacation. I commented on his excellent photography skills, and he agreed. But then he admitted, "One time I opened the camera by mistake and the whole roll of film got burned. So I don't do that anymore." Jonathan made a mistake, and then learned from that mistake. Isn't that what we want?

Remember Sam, the four-year-old with the Spiderman cape? Sam's mom allowed him to pick out his own clothes. Before allowing him to choose, his mom had decided that whatever Sam chose, she could live with the outcome. Sam had made his choice, and it had been a wrong choice. So what? Sam's mom had asked herself, "What's the worst that could happen if he wears a parka, boots and a Spiderman cape on a warm August morning?" Her answer was, "He might get warm and take them off." Her decision? "I can live with that."

Kids are smart. They know when they've made a mistake, and they learn from it. Sam, at four years old, was smart enough to realize that wearing a parka in August wasn't the right choice. He knew that he'd made a wrong choice, and he learned from it.

I tell my kids, when they've made a bad choice,
"That's okay.
We're going to learn from it and move on."
~Anita, mother of 2 kids and 1 teen

So, does this mean that you let your six-year-old make choices about when she is going to cross the street? Of course not! That's a health and safety issue. As parents, that's our department. Our kids don't get to make those choices. At every stage, you're in charge of your children's health and safety.

But whenever we can, we must allow our kids to make their own choices. We *want* our kids to make wrong choices sometimes. We *want* our kids to make mistakes sometimes. Because that's how they learn.

Last week, when our daughter got her driver's license,
she wanted to drive, all by herself, to her friend's house,
about 5 miles away. Even though I was really worried
about letting her drive by herself for the first time, I let
her. She survived and managed to get there and back
without me sitting next to her.
What do you know?
~Rhonda, mother of 1 kid and 1 teen

I guarantee you that the two-year-old who is allowed to choose between waffles and cereal becomes the teenager who makes better choices. I've seen it happen for 40 years. It's absolutely true.

THE TRUST BOX

When I was raising my kids, we had an imaginary Trust Box in our house. Here's how it worked: Every time one of my kids made a good choice, he or she earned some trust for the Trust Box. The more trust my kids accumulated in the Trust Box, the more independence they received. My kids learned that independence is earned; that it's a privilege, not a right.

Many families have a physical trust box, something like a glass vase or bowl that slowly gets filled with glass marbles as the trust is earned, so the kids can see how they're doing. I explain to both kids and parents that good decisions about anything (homework, rules, helping a sibling, getting to bed on time) earns trust and independence towards the things that they care about the most (staying up later, going to a party, being allowed to get a driver's license).

I once worked with Erika, a 15-year-old who was really struggling with her parents, resisting their rules and feeling that they didn't respect her. "It would be nice to be treated like an adult once in a while," she said. We then discussed how trust is earned, and that if she wanted to be treated like an adult, she had to act responsibly. I told Erika that to earn her parent's trust, she needed to follow her parents' rules, even if she didn't agree with every one of them.

Also, note that Erika had said, "...once in a while." She knew that she wasn't yet an adult, and she didn't want to live as an adult all the time. But she did have one foot in the adult world and wanted that to be acknowledged sometimes.

Allowing our child to make choices is an important element of teaching him to be a successful adult. Our role in this process is to make sure he knows what his options are, before he makes his choice. In order to do this, we've got to be able to communicate effectively with our child. In fact, good communication is essential for ALL relationships.

In the next chapter, I'll show you how to communicate effectively with your children AND with your parenting partner.

Chapter 6

EASY AND EFFECTIVE COMMUNICATION

Children don't need much advice,
but they really do need to be listened to,
and not just with half an ear.
~Emma Thompson, actress

Parents often tell me how difficult it is to get their kids to talk. And just as often, kids tell me how difficult it is to get their parents to listen. I'm here to tell you that good, fun and healthy communication doesn't have to be difficult; it can be easy and rewarding. Effective communication between parents and their kids—or between parenting partners— requires only two skills: listening and talking. It's really that easy.

Well, almost that easy. There is a bit more to it. First, we need to know *when* it's time to listen and *when* it's time to talk. Then, when we listen, we have to listen *carefully*. And when we talk, we have to talk *the way we'd like to be spoken to*.

LISTENING IS MORE IMPORTANT THAN TALKING

Listening is a magnetic and strange thing,
a creative force. The friends who listen to us
are the ones we move toward.
When we are listened to, it creates us,
makes us unfold and expand.
~Dr. Karl Menninger, founder of the Menninger Clinic

As parents, we do a lot of talking—to communicate tasks, express our intentions, establish rules, and keep our kids safe —but if we really want to nurture our relationships with our children, if we want them to share their thoughts and feelings openly with us, we need to do less talking and more listening.

Two ears and one mouth.

The most important element of communicating with our kids—and with anyone else, too, for that matter—is to remember that we have two ears and one mouth, and we should use them proportionately.

What we *hear* from our kids is more important than what we *say* to them. Besides, our kids already know what we're going to say, because we very often say the same things over and over again. It's important for us to be quiet and *listen.*

You have to be careful of what you say to your parents, because they take things so critically.
~Riley, 14 years old

We all want our kids and our teens to be able to talk with us, about anything, at any time, even if we're uncomfortable with the topic. But the only way our kids will feel comfortable talking with us is if they know we'll *listen* to them, that we won't yell at them, that we will be fair and calm. So we become expert listeners to anything our kids want to say. We also "listen" to their dreams, their interests, their friends, their music, and their actions.

As soon as you make it your priority to talk less and listen more, your children will notice, and they will soon be telling you more and more.

Besides, is there anyone on earth who you're more interested in, than your own kids?

One of my favorite things, is to listen to my daughter as she tells me about her day.
~Karla, mother of 1 teen

Listen with your full attention.

The most precious gift we can offer anyone
is our attention.
~Thich Nhat Hanh, Buddhist monk and teacher

Let's say that you're doing the dishes when your child comes up to you and says, "Mom! Mom! I want to tell you something!" You may be tempted to say, "Go ahead, tell me. I'm listening," and continue washing the dishes. But if you do that, you're not listening; you're doing the dishes. And your kid knows it.

Doesn't it make you angry, when your child (or partner) continues to type emails, offering the occasional, "Uh huh," when you're trying to talk to them? It makes you feel slighted and ignored. Your child feels the same way, when you keep your attention focused on doing the dishes, even though you say you're listening to her.

It's so much better, to give your child your full attention. If you can, turn off the water, dry your hands, turn to your child, make eye contact, and say to her, "Now tell me. I'm listening," and give her your full attention.

Or, if you really can't stop what you're doing at the moment, you can tell your child, "I really want to hear what you have to say. It's important to me, but I can't listen right now. I'll be done here in just a minute, and then I'll give you my full attention."

We need to teach our kids by example; we show them the right way to listen when we listen to them with our full attention.

Listen to understand.

Seek first to understand, and then to be understood.
~Stephen Covey, author and motivational speaker

Our kids want to be heard, and they especially want to be heard by their parents, who are two of the most important people in their life. But more than this, they want to know that we *understand* what they're telling us, that we understand them, that we *get* them.

Parents shouldn't take things so literally.
~Stephen, 13 years old

So many times, while someone is telling us something, we're thinking about how we're going to respond. We're planning our response, rather than fully paying attention to what they're saying, so that we can respond as soon as they stop talking. That's only half-listening, and it's not how we should listen to our children—or anyone else, for that matter.

When our child tells us something, we should *truly* listen and try to understand what he is saying. We'll have our chance to respond. But while our child is talking, we should be listening to both the words he is saying and also to the underlying messages that he is sending.

> **Parents need to listen more and give their child**
> **a chance to make their point, before they jump in.**
> ~Brianna, 14 years old

> **My son comes home from school**
> **and tells me everything at once.**
> **At first I was overwhelmed because I thought**
> **he wanted my advice or suggestions.**
> **But then I realized that all he wanted me to do**
> **was listen.**
> ~ Rebecca, mother of 1 teen

Try not to jump to conclusions about what you think your child wants. We often think we know the answers to the questions our children are asking, when in fact, we may not. We are often asked, "Dad, can I go to a party this weekend?" or "Mom can I sleep at my friend's house?" Before you respond with an answer, make sure you have the chance to speak with your child in private.

Ask him, "Are you hoping I say yes, or are you hoping I say no?" Sometimes, children feel socially pressured to ask their parents for permission to join a social activity, when they don't actually want to accept the invitation. I am always willing to be the bad guy. If my child says that she does not want to go, I'll say "Tell your friend that I say no." On the flip side, just because my child *does* want to attend, does not mean I will say yes.

A mother understands what a child does not say.
~Jewish Proverb

TALK TO YOUR CHILDREN THE WAY YOU WANT THEM TO TALK TO YOU

When you give respect, you get respect.
~Juan, father of 1 toddler and 1 kid

After a children's group swimming lesson, as I dressed two-year-old Alice in the locker room, another little girl kept turning the overhead lights off and on. Her mom said, "Stop it." When the little girl ignored her, the mom said, "Stop it!" again, more loudly. When the little girl continued to ignore her, the mom , "If you don't stop it we are not going to the park." The little girl looked at her mom and continued playing with the lights.

I looked at the little girl and said, "When you turn the lights off, I can't see what I'm doing, so I would appreciate it if you would please leave the lights on." She immediately stopped. She might have complied because I was a stranger who talked to her, but I'd like to think it was also because I politely explained to her *why* we needed the lights on. I spoke to her the way I would want someone to speak to me.

As their role models, we demonstrate for our children how to speak respectfully with other people, and how we would like to be spoken to. Why would we speak to our children any less respectfully than we want them to speak to others?

When we rail at our kids, they often don't listen to us. They think, "There goes Mom again, 'blah, blah, blah,'" and they tune us out. I believe that when we speak to our kids with respect, they will be more inclined to listen to us.

> ***When I speak rudely to my parents,***
> ***they speak rudely to me.***
> ~Erica, 14 years old

Sometimes we say to our kids, "Who taught you to talk that way?" Sometimes, *we* taught them to talk that way! We need to pay attention to the way we speak to our kids. If we want our kids to speak respectfully when they're adults, we should speak respectfully to them while we're raising them.

That doesn't mean always giving in. That doesn't mean being a friend. That doesn't mean being a pushover. It means being respectful. We can respectfully discipline our kids without sarcasm, without raising our voice, without being mean. We just talk to our kids the way we would like to be spoken to.

When my parents say, "Because I said so,"
I think they're abusing their adult authority.
It makes me feel like there's nothing
I can say, to stand up for myself.
I think I should always be given a good reason why.
Not, "Because I said so."
~Adam, 13 years old

One day, in a department store, I saw a dad walking ahead of his little boy, who was carrying something. The dad swung his arm back and accidentally knocked the item out of the little boy's hand. The dad whirled around and snapped, "Watch what you're doing!"

I was shocked. I thought, "This is not how to treat a child, or anyone else. Who else would he talk to like that?" The answer is, most likely, *nobody.* And certainly not to anyone he cares about. So why did he talk rudely to his son, whom he loves and whom he is teaching how to behave? Why do we do that?

When my dad yells at me,
I'm afraid of what he might say,
because he's not always the most supportive of me.
~Patrick, 13 years old

Yelling doesn't work.

Parents should not yell.
It just makes us scared and want to run away.
They get that look on their face and
we run away from that look.
~Drew, 7 years old

I'm going to make a confession: I used to be a yeller. My single, hard working mother was a yeller, and as a child, I was scared and sad when she yelled. I decided early on, "I'm never going to yell at *my* children." So guess what happened after I had my first child? I turned into a yeller, just like my mom. We tend to parent the way we were parented, and so despite my best intentions, I yelled.

Yelling is natural in my house;
we have a very loud house.
Angry yelling happens sometimes,
but it's usually directed at my little brothers,
rather than at me.
~Geoff, 14 years old

I'm proud to say that I've reformed. Here's what convinced me to change my screechy ways: One day, when my children were about seven and three years old, we were in the bathroom. I started yelling at them for doing something really horrible like refusing to brush their teeth. (You know, one of those minor issues that feels huge when it involves our child.) As I was yelling, I caught a glimpse of my face in the mirror, and had two horrifying thoughts: One was, "I look like my mom!" That was not a good thing. What woman wants to look like her mom?

The other was, "That is a really ugly, mean face. The only people in the world who ever see that scary face are my children: the people I love more than life itself, the most important people in the world to me, the people I would give my life for, the people I am teaching how to be good, kind adults."

At that very moment, I decided to make an effort to stop yelling. I didn't want that ugly, mean face to be what my kids thought of, when they thought of me. I told my children, that very night, that I was going to try very hard not to yell at them anymore, and that they could help me reach my goal by not yelling and by being good listeners. It was my job and my responsibility to stop yelling, but my children could help.

Even though it would make a great story, I wasn't able to stop cold turkey. Yelling is a tough habit to break, but I kept trying until I stopped. I put a rubber band on my wrist and wore it for about six months. Every time I started to yell or thought about yelling, I snapped the rubber band. Every time I saw it, it reminded me of what I was working on and to speak calmly and respectfully.

Yelling is a bad habit to get into; it's a good habit to get out of.

Yelling feels loud and annoying.
And it just makes me more nervous.
~Annelies, 5 years old

I'm not myself when people yell at me. I don't like it.
~Sarah, 13 years old

When my mom yells at my brother,
it stresses everyone out,
because then she gets in a bad mood,
and she gets mad at everyone else.
So it feels like she's yelling at me.
~Andrea, 13 years old

When my dad yells at me, I don't hear what he's saying, because I get all freaked out about it.
~Sophia, 14 years old

I have parents tell me, "But it's *hard* not to yell. It's *hard* to always say the right thing. It's *hard* to always be on our best behavior." And they're right. It is hard to be a good parent, to be calm when our buttons are being pushed, to say and do the right thing, especially when we're tired.

But isn't that what we expect from our kids? Don't we expect them to always be on *their* best behavior, to remain calm when they feel anything but calm, to make good choices, to do what they're told, to not yell at us? Why should we expect less from ourselves, than we expect from our children?

There are times when I want to hit my son, because he's being mean, rude, disrespectful, and the way he looks at me, as if I'm unbelievably stupid. It's hard for me to put up with his bad attitude, because when I grew up, kids didn't treat their parents that way.
~Wendy, mother of 1 kid and 1 teen

When our child yells or is rude to us, we feel irritated, so we might yell back or be rude to them. Then they feel irritated, and they respond by yelling or being rude....It's a vicious cycle, and it's up to us as parents to break it. After all, our kids are only doing what we've taught them to do.

When my parents yell at me, it makes me madder, and then I yell back at them.
~Amy, 14 years old

One trick for separating yourself from the strong negative emotions you might be feeling if your child has upset you, is to pretend, for the moment, that he is someone else's child. Seriously. Take a physical step backwards along with a deep breath, and say, "This is my neighbor's child." And then respond to your "neighbor's child" instead of to "your child." This takes much of your emotion out of the equation, and you'll be better able to speak calmly and rationally.

You take whatever emotion you're feeling and cut it in half. And that's the level of emotion you should show when you're frustrated with a kid.
~Alison, 20-year-old babysitter

BE EMPATHETIC

*I wish I could say to my mom, "I'm going through
a lot more than you can probably imagine.
If I'm rude or talking back, it's probably for a reason,
and if you took the time to listen, you'd understand
more, and see things from my point of view."*
~Brandon, 14 years old

Another element of communicating effectively with our children is to be empathetic, to look at the world through our children's eyes. Just a few words of empathy shows our kids that we value what they say.

Let them know you understand their feelings.

Imagine that you're a child who was not invited to a friend's birthday party. How would that make you feel? Now, imagine that you go home and tell your mother, "I didn't get invited to Patty's birthday party."

Let's compare two possible types of responses, one non-empathetic, and the other empathetic. In each case, pay attention to how you would feel, if your mother responded to you in these ways.

Non-empathetic response: "It's just a party. It's not that important. There'll be other parties."

Empathetic response: "Wow, I'm sorry. That's really disappointing."

How did the non-empathetic response make you feel? Your mother was doing her best to make you feel better, by downplaying the importance of the party. Did she succeed? Did you suddenly see the error of your ways and stop feeling sad? Did you feel that your mother understood your feelings?

How did the empathetic response make you feel? Did your mother's acknowledgement of your disappointment make you feel even sadder? Did her response make you feel as if she understood your feelings? Did that make you feel better?

Neither of your mother's responses got you invited to the party, but at least her empathetic words validated your feelings.

I was in a parent coaching session with a mom when her six-year-old daughter ran into the room and said, "Can we go miniature golfing?"

Mom offered a non-empathetic, "Of course not!" Her daughter responded by throwing a 10 minute tantrum. It would have been just as easy and so much better for the mother to offer a empathetic response, such as: "Oh, that's a fun thing to do. But it's too late today. Maybe we can plan that for another day."

My 6 year old daughter said, "I was so embarrassed."
I wanted to build her confidence,
so I said, "No, you weren't."
She said, "Oh, never mind!" and walked away.
Now I realize that my comment invalidated her feelings.
I should have said, "It doesn't feel good
when we are embarrassed. What happened?"
Then she would have stayed and talked.
~Adrienne, mother of 2 toddlers and 1 kid

Being empathetic can make your life easier, too, because if your kids know that you understand them, then they won't feel that they have to prove to you how much something means to them; they won't feel compelled to throw tantrums or act out or shout, "But it *is* important! It *is* a big deal!" This is a good thing.

So be empathetic. Let your kids know that you understand what they're thinking or feeling. You'll be amazed at how empathy and understanding will help you communicate with your kids.

Add a few more words.

Let's take a look at the following scenario:

Child: "Can I have a cookie?"

Parent: "No."

Child, crying: "But Mommy, I really, really want a cookie!"

Parent: "Oh come on, don't cry, it's just a cookie."

Child, stomping off to his room, "It's *not* just a cookie! I hate you!"

This conversation was a train wreck. The child ended up feeling unheard, the parent ended up feeling frustrated and conflicted ("Should I have let him have the cookie?"), and they both missed an opportunity for true communication. To the child, it *is* about more than just a cookie; it's also about being heard and having his feelings validated. Besides not having a cookie to enjoy, he's also frustrated because he can't make his mom understand his feelings, and he's sad because the most important person in the world (that would be his mom) doesn't get him. In fact, at some point, it isn't even about the cookie anymore.

Fortunately, there's an easy fix to these sorts of miscommunications: add a few more words. By adding a few words of empathy, the mother lets her child know that she understands his feelings, even though her answer is "no."

Let's replay the scenario with the parent adding some empathetic words to her answer:

Child: "Can I have a cookie?"

Parent: "Oh, a cookie does sound good, but now is not the time."

Child: "But I really want one!"

Parent: "Yes, I know, but it's too close to dinnertime. Maybe you can have one later."

Didn't this conversation go a lot better than the previous scenario? Even though the child may still be disappointed, he will at least know a couple of things: One, his mother empathizes with his desire for a cookie, and two, his mom is a good listener.

Let's say your 10-year-old comes home from school and says, "My teacher yelled at me today."

Your automatic response might be a non-empathetic, "What did you do, to make her yell at you?" This response will probably cause your child to become defensive; he might argue with you, storm off to his room mumbling about how his parents don't get him, or just clam up and not say any more about it. In any event, the result is a complete breakdown in communication.

Instead of responding immediately, why not take a few seconds to think of an empathetic response? Showing empathy doesn't imply that you think your child is blameless; it shows him that you understand how he feels about the situation.

An empathetic response might be, "Oh, that must've been difficult for you. What happened?"

Just a few words expressing empathy can make such a big difference in what your child will say next. A little bit of empathy can mean the difference between your child yelling back at you, "You never understand!" and your child saying, "Yeah, it was hard. Here's what happened..."

Be empathetic to your kids. Those few extra words of understanding say volumes to your child.

Let them have the last word sometimes.

I always find it interesting how long parents are willing to continue arguing with their kids. These arguments would end more quickly if we, the parent—the supposedly *mature* person—would stop arguing. Here is a typical argument between a 7-year-old boy and his dad:

Kid: "Hey Dad, did you know that cats can be purple?"

Dad: "No they can't."

Kid: "Uh huh. Alex said so."

Dad: "Well, Alex is wrong. Cats cannot be purple."

Kid: "Yes, they can."

Dad: "No, they can't."

The argument continues for awhile, with each side trying to convince the other that they are right, often with both sides getting louder and more annoyed.

Look at how much easier things would be, if the conversation went like this:

Kid: "Hey Dad, did you know that cats can be purple?"

Dad: "No they can't."

Kid: "Uh huh. Alex said so."

Dad: "Well, I have never seen a purple cat. But it sure would be cool to see one!"

Why not model how mature adults behave, by being the first one to stop arguing?

Silence is one of the hardest arguments to refute.
~Josh Billings, American humorist

As a coach, I often share meals with my clients, so that I can observe the family's interactions in their most comfortable setting. One night, a dad and his teenage daughter got into a yelling argument about her social plans for the following night, just as dessert was being served. After several loud and angry comments, the daughter yelled, "I am leaving!" and stomped down the hallway to her bedroom.

I was relieved; the room was quiet and the cake looked good. But the dad shouted, "Get back in here!"

Why, I wondered, did the dad demand his daughter return to the table? What possible benefit would it bring to the situation? My observation was that the daughter had acted in a mature way (ending the on-going argument), even if she did it in a rather immature way (storming off). The fact that the argument was over did *not* necessarily mean that the discussion was over. Dad could have eaten his dessert while everyone calmed down, and then gone to his daughter's room to calmly continue the discussion of whether his daughter was allowed to go to the party or not. Allowing his daughter to have the last word did *not* mean the father had allowed her to have her way.

THE THREE BEST PLACES TO TALK WITH YOUR KIDS

The three best places for talking with your kids are in the car, at bedtime, and at the dinner table. Let's take a look at why these places make such great places for conversation.

In the car.

My teenage daughter gets very embarrassed whenever the subject of sex comes up. But as her mom, I really needed to have some conversations with her about it. I saved these conversations for car rides when it was just the two of us. It was easier for her, because she didn't have to look at me, and I knew she couldn't escape.
~Olivia, mother of 1 teen and 1 kid

The car is a good place to talk with your kids for two reasons: one, your kids can't run away, and two, they don't have to make eye contact with you. Eye contact is difficult for some kids. When you're driving, hopefully you're not looking at your kids. You're watching where you're going, and your kids can be looking out the window. They don't have to make eye contact, so they're more comfortable talking with you.

And while we're on the subject of talking with your kid in the car, let's talk about *listening* with your kid in the car. If you don't already do it, consider carpooling. I always volunteered to help carpool with my kids and their friends. Carpooling is a great way to get to know your child's friends. By listening quietly, you'll learn what's going on in your child's group of friends, and beyond. You can learn who's doing what with whom, who is interested in what, and what the scoop is on a lot of different subjects. They know you're there, but if you're quiet for long enough, you tend to fade into the upholstery, as far as the kids are concerned, and they might relax enough to talk openly.

> *I've learned so much about my daughter and her friends, while driving them in my car. It sort of feels like I'm spying on them, but I'm not; they know I'm there.*
> ~Cynthia, mother of 1 teen

Also, whenever I had a choice between taking the kids somewhere or bringing them back home afterward, I always, *always*, offered to drive them home. Why? Because after an event, you get to hear how the activity *was,* rather than how they think the event will be. You get to hear who slow-danced with whom, whose dress was *way* too short, who sneaked alcohol into the party, who your daughter has a crush on. You get to hear things that otherwise you might not.

At bedtime.

Now that my children are teenagers, I really miss the time I spent with them as they were drifting off to sleep, when they were younger.
~ Sandra, mother of 2 teens

Talking at bedtime has the same benefits as talking in the car, plus your kid might be inclined to talk with you even longer. Why? Because your child is smart; he knows that bedtime is eight o'clock, but he's figured out that "If I start talking at eight, Mom and Dad will stay in here longer, and I'll get to stay up later."

When I tucked my children into bed at night, I would rub their backs and say, "Now tell me about your day." That's when I found out that they'd spilled their milk at lunch.

That's when I found out that they'd gotten in trouble at recess. That's when I found out that a friend had been mean to them. That's when you really find out what's going on in their lives. They're in their comfort zone, they're warm, safe and sleepy. Everything's calm and quiet. They feel loved. They feel safe opening up to you.

At the dinner table.

Family dinners have always been
an important element of our family culture.
In addition to being a time for the teaching of manners,
the sharing of conversation, and the eating of food,
it's also a time for just being together as a family.
~ Michael, father of 2 kids and 1 teen

The third good place to talk with your kids is at the dinner table. I believe that dinnertime is not primarily about nutrition. It's about family time. Dinnertime is a time for conversation. It's a time for connecting with each other. The conversation is much more important than the nutrition is. Sometimes we forget this.

One family shared their dinnertime tradition with me. Each person at the table gives their answer to an open-ended question, which changes each night. One night, the question might be, "Share something that you learned today." Another night, it might be, "Share one funny thing that happened today." Family members take turns choosing the question, and then listen when others share their stories. I think that's a great way to connect. You might try it. Or, you could come up with your own way to connect at dinnertime.

Now that you know the elements of good communication —listening well and speaking less; talking to people (our children included) the way we want to be spoken to; and expressing empathy—and how and when to enter into conversations, you are ready to learn how to build strong, lasting connections with your children—and with your parenting partner. I'll show you how to do that in the next chapter.

Chapter 7

BUILDING STRONG CONNECTIONS

Your family and your love must be cultivated like a garden. Time, effort, and imagination must be summoned constantly to keep any relationship flourishing and growing.
~Jim Rohn, business philosopher

The quality of the bonds we make with the other members of our family is critical to ensuring a healthy home environment, a nurturing atmosphere in which to raise our kids, a loving legacy, and the well-being of all involved. Let's take a look at how we can establish strong,lasting connections with our kids and with our parenting partner.

The bond that links your true family is not one of blood, but of respect and joy in each other's life.
~Richard Bach, author

BUILDING STRONG CONNECTIONS WITH YOUR KIDS

If I had my child to raise all over again,
I'd build self-esteem first, and the house later.
I'd finger-paint more, and point the finger less.
I would do less correcting and more connecting.
I'd take my eyes off my watch, and watch with my eyes.
I'd take more hikes and fly more kites.
I'd stop playing serious, and seriously play.
I would run through more fields and gaze at more stars.
I'd do more hugging and less tugging.
~Diane Loomans, author

Now that you know how to communicate effectively with your children, you can use these skills to build bridges between you and your children, bridges that will strengthen over time as your children grow up knowing that their parents not only love them, but will listen to them and try to understand them as well.

Here are some ways to build those bridges...

Ask your kids for their advice and their help.

A great way to interact with your kids is to ask them for their advice or their ideas. You might ask them, "What do you think about that?" or "Who would you vote for?" It's a great way to give your kids a chance to use their minds.

Ask them for their help, too. Kids love to help. I always asked my kids for help. I'm too short to reach the upper shelves of my kitchen cabinets, so whenever I needed to reach something, instead of getting the step stool, I'd say, "Hey, I need a kid to come help me." One would come in, and I'd put him, or her, on the counter, and they would reach what I needed.

Other times, I would loosen the jar of peanut butter just a little, and then I would say, "Hey, I need some help. I can't open the peanut butter. Could somebody come help me?" One of my kids would come in, and would be able to twist it open.

Asking your kids for their advice or help is great because it tells them that you need them and you trust them. It shows them they're important, valuable and capable members of a family. They get all those good messages when you say, "Hey, can you give me a hand?" or "What do you think about this?" or "What do you think we should do now?" Another positive result of asking your kids for their opinions is that it gives them practice making choices, which, as we discussed earlier, is a crucial skill for success as an adult.

Asking teens to educate us is another way to ask for advice. I once gave a 16-year-old boy, whom I did not know well, a ride home. His mother had advised me that he did not like to talk, and that I should not take it personally if he ignored me. Chuck and I got into my car, we buckled our seat belts, and I turned on the engine. Before I began driving, I turned to Chuck and said, "If I came to your high school, would I be able to find drugs?" Chuck began answering my question and did not stop talking for the 20 minutes it took us to get home. Teens are smart; they know a lot. Giving them the opportunity to share their knowledge is a great tool for building their self-confidence.

Spend time with your kids.

I have learned something over the years
about what children need most from their parents.
They need our time, measured not only in the number of
hours we spend with them each day,
but what we do with those hours.
~President Barack Obama

Someone once said, "The amount of time you spend with your children while they are growing up equals the amount of time they will spend with you while you're growing old."

Harry Chapin captured this in his song, "Cat's in the Cradle." They're right: one of the most important things we can do as a parent is to spend time with our kids. But not just so they'll he nice to us when you're old.

One of the secrets to a good parent-child relationship is spending time together. It's that simple. You may be thinking, "Susan, my kid's five. I spend every minute of every day with her." I know that's how it is now, but as our children get older, we tend to spend less and less time with them. It's crucial to spend time with your kids, no matter how old they are.

Children spell "love" ... T-I-M-E.
~Dr. Anthony P. Witham, author

My 27-year-old son called me last week and asked if I wanted to go to the movies. Of course I jumped at the opportunity! Now, why do you think he wanted to go to the movies with me? No, not just because I pay and order the large popcorn. It's also because going to the movies is something we started doing when he was three years old and it remains one of our favorite family activities.

I made it my priority to spend as much time as possible with my children, and that continues today. We spend time together, we hang out, we have fun. We do things *together*. That's the key.

Spending time with your kids doesn't just mean doing big things like going to Hawaii. (My kids are still waiting for their Hawaii trip.) It means watching a TV show together. It means having dinner together, or talking with them. It means walking to the coffee shop to get a donut on Saturday morning. It means simply being together, letting your children know how special they are to you.

Sometimes it's the boring things we remember the most.
~Russell, from the movie *Up*, referring to spending time with his dad

I used to love it,
when it was just my daddy and me in the house,
because we'd always have "daddy-daughter" time.
Now that my dad's remarried, we don't do that as much
anymore, so when we do now, it's really fun.
~Jessica, 14 years old

Want to indulge your child?
Spend, spend, spend...
Time.
~CitiBank Television Commercial

The more time you spend with your kids, the better you get to know them, and the better they get to know you. I wanted my kids to understand that I'm not just Mom, I'm also Susan. I'm a person. I have interests. I have emotions. I have a personality.

A mom called me for advice because she and her 13-year-old daughter weren't getting along. They argued all the time, mostly over small, silly things. "Your daughter is looking for more attention from you," I suggested. "She's asking for more of your time."

"How do I even start?" the mom asked.

I said, "Why don't just the two of you go out to dinner? Leave your husband and your son at home, and go have a girls' only dinner."

After a pause, she said, "You know what? I haven't gone out to dinner alone with my daughter in probably five years."

She started making weekly dates to go out to dinner with her daughter. The girl is now 18, and their relationship is awesome. They understand each other, they know each other, and they appreciate each other.

I feel like I spend enough time with my parents.
I go to the movies with my mom,
and sometimes shopping or for walks.
I like hanging out with her.
~Ariana, 13 years old

Sometimes on the weekends,
I go to the movies with my mom.
I'd go with my dad more, if he didn't always want
to see action movies, which are boring.
~Jennifer, 12 years old

Sometimes when I get out of school early, my mom will
take me to a park, where we'll have sandwiches.
~Debbie, 10 years old

Every weekend I go grocery shopping with my dad.
It's kind of been our thing since I was
about five years old.
~Tina, 15 years old

I like spending time with my parents, for the most part.
But sometimes it gets annoying, if I spend too much time
with them, because they get on my nerves.
~Jeff, 12 years old

I like spending time with my dad.
He gets stressed out a lot, and when he spends
time with me, he calms down.
~Melanie, 13 years old

I spend a lot of time with my mom. We're really close.
We're more like sisters than like a mother and daughter.
We go out and have fun.
~Felicia, 16 years old

We are active with Cub Scouts, we have play dates,
we go berry-picking, hiking, to amusement
parks, to restaurants, and on family vacations.
Given the choice, I like to spend time
with the entire family (kids plus husband),
more than with kids alone.
~Sabrina, mother of 1 toddler and 1 kid

I love spending time with my children.
We just like to hang out together.
I am very aware of how little time I have left
with them at home. I am a stay-at-home mom and
I am very lonely when they are not around.
~Marilyn, mother of 2 teens

I am a stay-at-home mom, so I spend A LOT of time with
my kids. I do wish I had more time for myself.
~Cynthia, mother of 2 kids

I'm trying to find ways to get more one-on-one time
with each of my kids. Right now each of them is working
on a different behavior chart, and their reward
is an ice cream date with Dad.
Hopefully that will mean lots of ice cream for me!
~Jeff, father of 3 kids

We all eat breakfast and dinner together every day.
Dinner is especially important. We all sit together
and talk and really listen to each other.
It is such a great chance to just be with them
and enjoy talking with them.
~Emily, mother of 2 kids

BUILDING STRONG CONNECTIONS WITH YOUR PARTNER: PARENTING AS A TEAM

One of my least favorite parts of parenting is arguing with my husband over how to handle our son's behavior issues.
~Marybeth, mother of 1 kid

One of the trickiest relationships to navigate within a family is the relationship between parenting partners. Having a parenting partner can make some aspects of parenting easier (as any single parent will attest), but it also has the potential to make other parts of life quite difficult.

When parenting partners disagree.

The question, "What do I do when my partner doesn't want to do something the way I want to do it?"comes up at every one of my presentations. It's a big issue, and it carries a lot of emotional baggage. It's an issue that makes parents question their partner's common sense, their trust in each other and their ability to work as a team.

I met with a couple recently who were having problems working together as a parenting team. Their conversation sums up what a lot of parenting partners experience:

"Before we had kids," the wife said, "we never argued. We sailed along, solving problems together and getting along really well. Then we had kids, and everything changed."

"Now," the husband added, "every time an issue comes up with one of our kids, I want to do things one way, and my wife wants to do it another. Parenting our kids correctly is *extremely* important to both of us. And yet, we can't ever agree on how to proceed."

"That's right," the wife agreed. "We both seem to be locked into our own patterns and beliefs of how things should be done, certain that our way is the right way. I often wonder where my sensitive, intelligent partner has gone. That can't be good for a marriage—or for our kids."

When partners frequently disagree with each other, it can make them question their entire relationship. Our emotions are heightened around issues with our children, and things get more complicated and more emotional when we do not feel supported by our partners.

Disagreeing with our partner about parenting issues is one of the least fun parts of being a parent, and also one of the most common. Our parenting style is a complex, highly individualized interplay of many elements, including our temperament, our passion about or interest in the issue, our patience level, our reaction to the way we were raised and even our mood at the moment. In light of this, it should seem more surprising that any two people *could* parent identically. And yet, that's often what we expect from our parenting partner.

I'm not sure why people think that they will agree with their partner about every parenting issue. We fall in love despite (or maybe because of) our differences, not just because we share similarities. We have different tastes in food, hobbies, and friends. We have different political and religious views, and we were raised differently by different parents in different cities or countries. Is it all that surprising that our views of parenting may also differ?

There is nothing inherently wrong when two parents disagree. It is a natural, normal and expected result of having two different people approach an issue. It's okay if children know their parents disagree. In fact, it could be used as an opportunity to role model conflict resolution. Children can learn from watching their parents disagree, calmly discuss the issue and reach a solution together. What is *not* okay is to argue in front of children. It's scary for them, and can make them worry about the solidity and security of their family.

Sometimes a child will ask her parents a question at the dinner table, and both parents answer at the same time, one with a resounding "No" and one with a resounding "Yes." When this happens, the appropriate response would either be for the parents to calmly discuss the issue—possibly with more input from their child—and resolve it right then and there, or, if the issue was one that the parents felt strong disagreement about, they might tell their child that they would discuss the issue in private and get back to her with the answer later.

Would I want to be consulted?

One issue that causes many parental conflicts is when one parent responds to a child's question without consulting the other parent. The parent who is not consulted often feels left out and unimportant. Their authority feels diminished and they often feel angry. When your child asks you a question, and your partner isn't present, ask yourself, "Is this a decision I would want to be involved with?" If it is, then you owe it to your partner not to answer your child's question at that time, but rather to say, "I'm going to wait until you and I can discuss this with Mom/Dad, and then we will come up with an answer as a family."

It can be very helpful to discuss with your partner in advance how you feel about certain issues, and how you will, as a team, handle those issues. But there will always be issues that you disagree about. *So simply agree to disagree.* Accept that there will be times when you will get your way, and there will be times when you are willing to step back and allow things to go your partner's way. Make sure that the parent who gets their way, gets to handle the entire situation. For instance, if one parent feels that the children should be allowed to stay up late to watch a TV show, then that parent also gets to deal with the children in the morning!

THE THREE "L'S" OF HAPPY PARENTING: LAUGHING, LIVING, LOVING

Parents are often so busy
with the physical rearing of children,
that they miss the glory of parenthood,
just as the grandeur of the trees is lost
when raking leaves.
~Marcelene Cox, writer

Laugh More!

One of my favorite parts of parenting is
hearing the funny things my kids say.
~Henry, father of 3 kids

Our kids are really funny. They're bright, they're clever and they're cute. The problem is that sometimes we get so serious, so wrapped up in parenting, that we forget to laugh. If our kid does something that we don't expect, we may not think it's funny. But it may be really funny to everyone else. Don't you laugh when other people's kids do something funny?

I was talking at a preschool one night, and a mom told me, "I don't know what to do when my son calls me a 'Poopy Mommy'." She was very serious, but everybody else in the room burst out laughing. One of the suggestions I made to her was that she make a joke out of it, and laugh along with her son.

I love to laugh with my kids,
to experience their undiluted joy.
~Marlene, mother of 2 kids

Kids are funny. Life is funny and way too short. We need to relax and laugh more. Humor is a very important element of family life, and of life in general.

Lighten Up!

At the end of the day, I feel like I'm doing the best I can.
It's enough.
~Justine, mother of 3 kids

We should all stop what we're doing, take a deep breath and RELAX! I know that parenting is hard work, but that doesn't mean we can't be relaxed. The best parents aren't necessarily the ones who are tense all the time. Being tense is not good for us, or for our kids. We need to remember to lighten up, and have more fun.

I get bogged down in the negative, sometimes,
and it's really hard to see the positive in my kids.
Sometimes, it's hard for us; as parents,
we tend to focus in on that one negative thing,
and forget about all their really nice qualities.
~Pete, father of 3 kids

We forget, sometimes, that we moms need playdates, too.
~Yvonne, mother of 4 kids

You don't always have to be the serious parent. You can have a good time. Be silly with your kids. They'll love it! When you take your kids to the park, go down the slide with them, hop on the swing next to them and just have fun! You have my permission. And your kids will appreciate it.

At a birthday party for a three-year-old, a large platter of cookies tempted every child who walked through the kitchen on their way to the backyard. As I watched, every child who came by asked, "Can I have a cookie?"

And every parent said, "No, you need to eat lunch first."

It took all my will power not to shout, "Oh, just give the kid a cookie! You're at a party; relax and have fun!"

It would have been totally appropriate for Mom or Dad to say, "Yes, you may have a cookie. Since we're at a party, we are going to be silly and eat a cookie before lunch. At home, we wait until after lunch. But today, it's okay. And thank you for asking first."

I'm going to give you permission to stop working so hard at parenting. You know all that planning and organizing and scheduling and car pooling and driving and shopping and controlling and expecting and hoping and worrying you do? It's hard work! I want you to know that it's okay to relax a little; all the important stuff will still get done.

In fact, if you relax, you'll even have time for some more important activities with your kids, activities that you might have been neglecting—like hugging or eating lunch together in the park or reading a book together. You're working way too hard, so relax a bit and try to enjoy parenting more.

I feel a tremendous responsibility for helping these little precious people become kind, loving, responsible adults. I never stop worrying about them or stop loving them.
~Ariana, mother of 2 kids

I also want to give you permission to stop worrying so much. As parents, we tend to worry about everything. We started worrying about our kids before they were even born! By the time my firstborn was six months old, I had thrown away all the child development books, because depending on which book I was reading, I was either raising the next Einstein or the next Rain Man and I didn't want to deal with that.

So I looked at my six month-old and I said, "You know what? He's perfect just the way he is. He's moving forward, he's progressing and that's good enough for me." That's when I tossed the books.

And while we're on the subject of lightening up, don't forget to lighten up on your kids. We need to stop expecting so much from our kids. These days, in addition to going to school five days a week, a typical kid may also go to religious school and language school and be on the soccer team. In the spring, she's on the softball team and three afternoons a week, during the school year, she goes to a tutoring center to help her get ahead in her classes. In the summer, she goes to summer school, so she won't forget what she learned during the school year. When does she get to have fun?

Kids often have a long list of activities, and many parents expect their kids to excel at everything they do. They can't just go to school: they have to get straight A's. They can't just play soccer: they have to play on a competition team. It's even worse for our teenagers: they can't just get straight A's, they have to get straight A's *in the AP classes.*

The stresses of school and impending college
are overwhelming—and I feel the way things are set up,
if your child is not getting all "A's"
he has no hope of going to college.
I have been to several college night seminars
and have seen parents crying in the hall!
~Robert, father of 2 teens

Here's a secret: *Your kids really don't have to do all this, in order to become successful adults!* We need to back off and allow our kids to develop at their own pace, with their own interests, in their own way. If your kid is on the baseball team, he doesn't also have to go to the baseball coach for extra practice once a week. He doesn't have to be a starter on the team. He can just play baseball for fun. What a concept! We need to remember that life is supposed to be fun... especially for kids.

Say "I love you" every day.

One of my favorite things about parenting is sharing unconditional love with my child.
~Mary, mother of 1 kid

Please say "I love you" to your children at least once, every day. You love them with all your heart; you should let them know it. They need to hear it, and often. Don't ever assume that they've heard it enough, even if they tell you they have.

It's especially good to say, "I love you," to your kids after they've misbehaved, when they don't feel very lovable. They need reassurance that we still love them even when they're not on their best behavior.

I try to end every conversation with my kids by saying, "I love you." And they say the same thing right back at me. Having your kids say, "I love you, too," makes all the hard work worth it. All the laundry and cooking and arguing and worrying and driving seems worth it, when my children say —and mean—"I love you Mom".

In order to build strong connections with our kids, it's important for us to ask them for their input, to listen to them and to spend time with them. We build stronger bridges with our parenting partner when we accept that we may disagree from time to time, and we use one or more of the tactics suggested here—agreeing to disagree, working toward an acceptable solution, allowing your partner to have his or her way sometimes, making sure to consult your partner on issues that you feel would be important to him or her—in order to resolve the disagreement.

And finally, remember to Laugh More! Lighten Up! and Say "I love you," Every Day! because happy parents make happy families.

Chapter 8

NOW GO OUT THERE AND HAVE FUN

The rules for parents are but three...
love, limit, and let them be.
~Elaine M. Ward, author

Before I had my first baby, I had worked with children, spent time with children, and loved children for over 16 years. I knew how to change diapers, prepare bottles and rock babies to sleep. I knew how to calm distraught toddlers whose parents had left for a little while, and care for pre-schoolers who were ill. I knew how to help children with homework, how to resolve issues among siblings and how to make kids feel special. I knew how to listen to teenagers and help them with tough decisions.

Was I prepared to have a baby of my own? Absolutely! Or so I thought...

When I brought Brandon home, reality hit. Parenting was *much* harder than babysitting or teaching. Parenting was—and is—the toughest job I've ever done. This is a no-end-in-sight, without-a-break, 24-7, FOREVER job. During the first few sleepless months, Brandon's father would occasionally ask, "When are his parents coming to get him?" He was only joking...I think.

Don't over-parent.

Yes, parenting is a very hard job. But then we go and make it harder than it needs to be...

We don't have to monitor our child's every move.

We don't have to count the bites of food our child takes and be concerned if the number is two instead of seven.

We don't need our child to be well-behaved every minute.

We don't have to come up with a solution to "I'm bored!"

We don't have to fill our child's every moment with a scheduled activity.

We don't have to worry about an occasional missed homework assignment or a low grade on a quiz.

We don't have to hold a mediation session every time our children bicker with each other.

We don't have to worry if one child has fewer friends than her sibling.

We make ourselves *crazy*, by over-thinking, over-reacting, over-worrying every parenting decision—by *over-parenting*.

Elements of good parenting.

As a good parent, there are certain things we must do. We must make our child's safety our top priority in our minds and in our homes. We must make sure that their environment is safe, that we're watching our children when they need supervision, and that we're careful when leaving our children in the care of others.

Good parenting means putting our children first, all the time. It means considering our children's needs and schedules before our own. It means being willing to adjust our plans at the last minute, when our children's needs require us to.

Good parenting means taking care of ourselves, as well. It means occasionally plopping the kids in front of the television for thirty minutes so we can take a much-needed and well-deserved break. It means participating in an exercise program, taking a class, joining a book club, or being involved in any other pursuit that keeps our mind and body in tune, even if it means leaving our child with a babysitter. Sometimes it means bringing home take-out food, instead of preparing a home-cooked dinner.

It also means having regularly-scheduled date nights with our partner, so we get a much-deserved break from parenting and a chance to remind each other why we chose to live together all those years ago—which can be difficult to remember amidst crying babies, arguing children, and disagreements at 3:30 a.m. about whose turn it is to get up to change a diaper or check on the noise coming from our teen's room.

Good parenting also means making sure your children know that they are the most important people in the world to you. I used to tell Casey, "You are the best little girl in the world…to me. Every mommy thinks her little girl is the best. But to me, you are." I wanted my children to know they were special to me, but I did not want them to be conceited, or to believe that they were really special to anyone other than me.

Children who believe that they are loved, valued and important have higher self-esteem, more confidence, and act more loving toward others, than those who were not raised to believe that about themselves

Remember that the more a child feels valued, the better his values will be.
~Anonymous

Good parenting means sometimes saying "No," even when our children are hoping for "Yes." It means setting rules, being strict and sounding like our parents used to sound, even though we promised ourselves we never, ever would. It means putting boundaries around our children until they're old enough and wise enough to create and respect their own limits and those of society.

Good parenting means allowing our children to fail and to be frustrated even when it breaks our heart to see them in tears. It means allowing them to be disappointed, to fail a test, to not be invited to a birthday party. It means NOT rescuing them from every emotional pain, so they learn how to rescue themselves.

Good parenting also means laughing more. Laughing feels good and it's good for us, too. Humor is a wonderful tool for diffusing bad moods, distracting toddlers from an impending temper tantrum and teaching your kid that not everything is a problem. It's more difficult to feel annoyed when we're laughing, and it's more difficult to stay grouchy when we're smiling.

Laughter is the shortest distance between two people.
~Victor Borge, comedian and musician

Parenting is fun!

Parenting IS fun. Parents get to splash in puddles, draw in coloring books (outside the lines if you want), ride a merry-go-round, read *Goodnight Moon* a thousand times, giggle loudly and often, and snuggle at bedtime. Dads get to participate in teddy-bear picnics without losing their man card, and moms get to play in the dirt without worrying about their nails. And as our children grow, it's so rewarding and thrilling to hear their opinions, their thoughts, and their dreams. Watching our babies develop into toddlers, kids, teens, and finally young adults is a true joy every day.

As parents, we have to try to be the best that we can be, every single day. That doesn't mean we have to be perfect—it means we simply have to try our best. If we make some less-than-great parenting decisions, we should learn from them, let them go, and move on.

Even the best parents make mistakes. Our kids forgive us when we make mistakes, and we forgive them when they make mistakes; we should forgive ourselves, as well. When we make a parenting mistake,we should figure out how to do better next time, and we should apologize to our children. How else will they learn the value of an apology?

Every day, we get another chance to make better decisions, to be a better parent, and to enjoy parenting more. Isn't that wonderful?

When we become a parent, we get the gift of accompanying our child through every age, every stage, every experience and every challenge. Yes, our children give us sleepless nights, challenges, worry, stress and frustration, but they also fill our lives with joy, fun, laughter, hope and love. I wouldn't have it any other way. Would you?

In the end, that's what being a parent is all about:
those precious moments, the times we spend
with our children that fill us with pride
and excitement for their future;
the chance we have to set an example
or offer a piece of advice
or just be there to show that we love them.
~President Barack Obama

4907301R00109

Made in the USA
San Bernardino, CA
15 October 2013